ויברכם ה' אלכון

Avraham Hertz

THE HOLY CITY

Jews on Jerusalem

THE B'NAI B'RITH JEWISH HERITAGE CLASSICS

Series Editors: DAVID PATTERSON · LILY EDELMAN

ALREADY PUBLISHED

THE MISHNAH
Oral Teachings of Judaism
Selected and Translated by Eugene J. Lipman

RASHI
Commentaries on the Pentateuch
Selected and Translated by Chaim Pearl

A PORTION IN PARADISE
And Other Jewish Folktales
Compiled by H. M. Nahmad

*Published in cooperation with the Commission
on Adult Jewish Education of B'nai B'rith.*

THE HOLY CITY

Jews On Jerusalem

Compiled and Edited by

AVRAHAM HOLTZ

W · W · NORTON & COMPANY · INC · NEW YORK

FIRST EDITION
SBN 393 04327 4
Library of Congress Catalog Card No. 75-78069
ALL RIGHTS RESERVED
Published simultaneously in Canada
by George J. McLeod Limited, Toronto

Printed in the United States of America

1 2 3 4 5 6 7 8 9 0

For My Mother

"Give her of the fruit of her hands,
and let her works praise her in the gates."

(Proverbs 31:31)

Contents

Preface

Throughout the many centuries of exile, Jews have always lived on two planes—the one into which they were thrown by the accidents of history, and the other, Jerusalem, considered by the sages as the center of the universe, to which they were drawn by longing and by faith.

Cartographers may fix the city's location at 31° 46′ 45″ north latitude and 35° 13′ 25″ east longitude. Geographers may chart Jerusalem's terrain and record its climate. Archeologists may retrieve civilizations buried in its mountains, and historians may study the ruins in search of its past. But Jewish poets who sing of Jerusalem know that its sublimity, like the divine essence, must remain ineffable. For who can adequately transcribe the joy and grief that this city has inspired in Jews regardless of when or where they lived? The same impulse that compels man to laud God's greatness has motivated Jewish writers in every age to celebrate the loving attachment of the people to the city. While extolling Jerusalem's beauty, they expressed each generation's faith in the eternal promise. They obstinately denied the rights and titles of the numerous conquerors who, with rare exception, ravaged the city, harassed its inhabitants, and tarnished its splendor.

The purpose of this anthology is to illustrate the centrality of Jerusalem in Jewish history and tradition from earliest days to the immediate present. To this end, an attempt has been made to present views of the city through relevant and illuminating passages from Jewish sources ranging from the Bible through reactions to the Six-Day War of June, 1967.

The book begins with selections from the Hebrew Bible, which

11

is our principal literary source for Jerusalem's origins and its first and lasting impact on the Jewish people. In the first chapter, the early history is rounded out with selections from the Apocrypha and from Josephus.

The four succeeding chapters deal with the genres of literature predominant in transmitting a sense of the importance of Jerusalem to the oncoming generations. During the rabbinic era, which has exerted the most profound effect in shaping Jewish character and destiny, the law (Chapter 2) and lore (Chapter 3) of Judaism were forged. During this period, which witnessed the rebuilding and the destruction of the Second Temple, liturgy (Chapter 4) also played a major role. After the dispersion of the Jews to the far corners of the earth, travelers to Zion (Chapter 5) left a wealth of documentation about Jerusalem, particularly during the Middle Ages.

Chapter 6 deals with the modern period, with stress on the literature of Zionism and the early pioneers who built a Jewish homeland in Palestine. The volume concludes with materials related to the Six-Day War of June, 1967, which resulted in the capture by the Israelis of the Old City and the reunification of Jerusalem.

I wish to acknowledge a special editorial debt arising from my absence abroad on sabbatical leave while this manuscript was being readied for the printer. Dr. David Patterson and Mrs. Lily Edelman, editors of the Jewish Heritage Classics Series, had the difficult and time-consuming tasks of checking and rearranging much of the material to bring it into its present form. I would also like to thank Mr. and Mrs. Milton T. Smith of Austin, Texas, for their generous assistance.

A. H.

Neveh Schechter
Jerusalem
November, 1969

Introduction

Jerusalem is the heartland of Judaism. Jews have never ceased to proclaim their attachment to the Holy City—in vision and prayer, homily and Psalm, in travelers' tale and poem, in testimony and reminiscence. For almost three thousand years the Jewish people have woven Jerusalem into the innermost texture of their communal life, their religion and culture. The Western Wall, symbolizing the ancient glory of the Temple, remains Judaism's most revered and hallowed site.

Since very early in the history of Christianity Jerusalem has also been sacred to the Christian world, and the city is usually illustrated in Christian maps as the center of the earth. Long before Christianity became an official religion of the Roman Empire, a Christian community lived in Jerusalem, while the Jews were denied the right to live in, or even visit, their most sacred city. With the imperial toleration of Christianity, Jerusalem underwent a revival, greatly aided by Constantine's mother, St. Helena, who sponsored a large amount of building there in the fourth century; the city has been a center for pilgrims ever since. Everywhere in Old Jerusalem there are sites traditionally connected with events in the life of Jesus and of many saints. In the Christian quarter, for example, there are the Church of the Holy Sepulchre and the Via Dolorosa, over which Jesus is said to have carried his cross.

After the Arab conquest in 637 c.e. Jerusalem became the chief Moslem shrine after Mecca and Medinah. Many places of worship were established, sometimes on the sites of former Jewish and Christian monuments. The sacred enclosure, the *Haram ash-Sharif,* built on the Temple site of Mount Moriah, contains the Dome of

13

the Rock, or Mosque of Omar, and the Mosque known as *Al-Masjid al-Aqsa,* both of which are outstanding examples of Moslem architecture.

The name of the city first occurs as *Urusalim* as early as the nineteenth century B.C.E. in the Egyptian Execration texts and in the fourteenth-century tablets from Tell el-Amarna; then as *Urusalimu* in the Assyrian records of Sennacherib. These forms are, in fact, almost identical with the Hebrew and Aramaic *Yerushalim* or *Yerushalem* and have the same meaning: "the foundation of (the god) Shalem (prosperer)." In addition to the form *Beit Shalem,* which is also found in the Amarna tablets, there is the abbreviation *Shalem* (Salem). Jerusalem is also referred to as Moriah, Zion, City of God, City of the Great King, and City of David. For a time the Roman city, built by Hadrian in 135 C.E. to replace the one destroyed by Titus sixty-five years previously, bore the name *Aelia Capitolina.* Arabs know the city as *Al Quds.* But for the Jew, the name which strikes the clearest emotional chord is *Yerushalayim.*

Jewish history in Jerusalem began with David's conquest of the Jebusite city about 1000 B.C.E. With this act David accomplished two major goals: he removed a pocket of Canaanite resistance, and he established a centrally located, autonomous capital which belonged neither to the northern tribes of Israel nor to the southern tribe of Judah. Throughout the entire Biblical period the city was known as "the City of David," a royal holding that passed on to the Davidic kings. Hence, pre-exilic writers generally speak of Judah *and* Jerusalem. So, too, in a list of the exiles, Jerusalemites are referred to separately (see Jeremiah 52:28–30).

By transferring the Ark of the Covenant to the city and by setting up residence there, David made Jerusalem the political capital, the royal domicile, and the foremost Israelite sanctuary. From that date onward ancient Israelite doctrine cemented the association of Zion and David: as David and his heirs were selected by the Lord to reign in perpetuity, so was Jerusalem chosen as His earthly abode forever.

The construction of the Temple, undertaken by Solomon (960–

922 B.C.E.), was the most elaborate and ambitious of that monarch's building projects: it took seven years to complete. In addition, Jerusalem housed magnificent palaces, an armory, and a court. These structures, together with Jerusalem's natural beauty, made it a picturesque city: "the perfection of beauty."

After the dissolution of the union of Judah and Israel, the kings of Israel attempted to divert their people's love for Jerusalem to other sanctuaries, but it was in vain. Even after the destruction of the First Temple we read that "there came certain men from Shechem, from Shiloh, and from Samaria, even fourscore men, having their beards shaven and their clothes rent, and having cut themselves, with meal offerings and frankincense in their hands to bring them to the house of the Lord" (Jeremiah 41:5). The cities mentioned are all in the north, in what was "Israel," thus indicating that even from the northern centers the people gravitated to Jerusalem. This text also attests to the fact that Jews visited Jerusalem even after the destruction of the Temple.

After the secession, Jerusalem's fate was contingent upon the achievements or debacles of Judah's rulers. In times of peace and prosperity the city flourished; in times of strife and disturbance it experienced privation. Frequently the Temple's gold and silver utensils were stripped to pay the price of defeat or vassalage; its walls were damaged and in constant need of repair.

After the reign of Menasseh (687–642 B.C.E.), who had acceded to Assyria's demand and introduced foreign worship into the Temple, Josiah (640–609), sensing Assyria's eventual fall, embarked upon a series of religious reforms. These reached a climax in 622 when the "Book of the Torah" was discovered and promulgated as the law of the land. In a public ceremony in Jerusalem the people pledged themselves to obey the Torah and eradicate foreign cultic practices. The Temple was repaired and rededicated. With the centralization of the Israelite cult, Jerusalem regained its prestige and sanctity.

In 605 King Jehoiakim became a Babylonian subject under Nebuchadnezzar. On Jehoiakim's death, Jehoiachin ascended the throne. Hoping for Egyptian aid, he rebelled in 598, as a result of which he was deported together with the city's nobility. (This was known as "the exile of Jehoiachin.") Zedekiah remained loyal until 589 when he revolted in spite of the prophet Jeremiah's warning to capitulate. By January, 588, Jerusalem was under siege. When the siege was lifted that summer, the citizens of Jerusalem were temporarily relieved, although Jeremiah continued to predict total catastrophe. In July, 587, the Babylonians broke through the walls and entered the city. Three weeks later, Nebuzaradan arrived in Jerusalem and was instructed to set fire to the city and level its walls. The foremost citizens were deported to Babylon.

Before the destruction the city's population had probably never exceeded thirty thousand. Little information is available about the number of Jews in Jerusalem during the fifty years between the destruction and the First Return. Since the exiles found a native Jewish population there on their return, it seems reasonable to assume that a small number of refugees from Jerusalem had trickled back to the city. We also know that pilgrims did continue to visit the holy sites and that there later arose a cadre of "Mourners for Zion and Jerusalem," who lived in self-abnegation and prayed for the city's deliverance.

As Babylon's power waned, the Persian Empire under Cyrus, acclaimed by Deutero-Isaiah as "God's anointed," extended its dominion. During the first year (538) of his reign in Babylon, in conformity with his policy to permit conquered peoples to maintain their religions and cultures, Cyrus ordered the restoration of the Jewish Commonwealth and the rebuilding of the Temple. Assisted by Jews in Babylon and Egypt, a large contingent of Jews returned; but, beset by enemies, impoverished, and dejected, the people delayed the construction of the Temple for two decades. It was finally dedicated and the walls temporarily repaired. About a century later, under the rule of Ezra and Nehemiah, the civil administration was reorganized, the religious life revitalized, and Jerusalem was once again recognized as the unrivaled center of Jewish culture. Having been granted semiautonomous rule within the Persian Empire, the leaders levied taxes and struck coins. Seal impressions dating from the fourth century B.C.E. bear the imprint "Yehud" or "Yerushalem."

From the time of Alexander the Great, who conquered the area in 332, and his successors, the Ptolemies and Seleucids, Hellenistic civilization spread through the East, and Greek city-states were founded in the wake of the armies. The Seleucid monarch Antiochus IV (175–163 B.C.E.) embarked upon a program to unify his kingdom culturally, imposing upon his subjects the worship of the Olympian Zeus and of his own image as the god's living manifestation. His designs were promoted in Jerusalem by the hellenized High Priest Jason, who hastened to establish a *gymnasium* there. Scholars claim that such *gymnasia,* always identified with pagan worship, were organized as legally independent corporations with specific rights. Many Jews denounced the Jerusalem *gymnasium* and ostracized its members.

In 169 B.C.E., aided by Menelaus, the new High Priest, the king raided the Temple. Two years later he made the citizens of the city dependent upon the Acra, a walled citadel built on one of the hills west of Jerusalem and organized as a Greek *polis,* where hellenized foreigners and Jews lived under their own constitution. Regular sacrifices were prohibited, and the observance of circumcision and of Sabbath and Festivals was barred. In December, 167, an altar to Olympian Zeus was erected in the Temple court. Three years of Jewish guerrilla resistance culminated in Judas Maccabeus' march into Jerusalem, where he surrounded the Acra and cleansed the Temple, rededicating it in 164. The event is still celebrated in the Festival of Ḥanukkah. Subsequently the walls were rebuilt, and by 142 Simon, Judas' brother, secured the country's absolute independence.

With the Roman conquest, the area was divided into five provinces and Jerusalem became the capital of one of them. King Herod beautified the city and began a reconstruction of the Temple, which was completed in 62 C.E. During the second Commonwealth it is estimated that Jerusalem's population may have reached two hundred thousand. Leading to the city were twelve roads, which were repaired annually in order to accommodate the Jewish pilgrims who flocked there for the Festivals. In 70 both city and Temple were destroyed.

Hadrian (117–138), who rebuilt the city as a Roman metropolis (*Aelia Capitolina*) and converted the Temple site into a center for the cult of Jupiter Capitolinus, imposed severe restrictions upon the Jews. Though defeated and humiliated, the Jews arose in 132, and, under Bar Kokhba, liberated Jerusalem and made it the seat of government for three years. Coins have been found from this period bearing the imprint "Jerusalem" and "Year One of Israel's Freedom."

Though Jews were legally barred from Jerusalem, many sources suggest the prohibition was never strictly observed. Even under Constantine, when the city became a Christian sanctum and Jewish residence was theoretically banned, Jews openly lived in the city. Under Emperor Julian (355–363), the Jews were encouraged to rebuild the Temple. But Julian's death crushed the reawakened hope for redemption, which had prompted many Jews to return to Jerusalem and take part in its resuscitation.

About a century later, for some unexplained reason, Jewish hopes for Jerusalem's reclamation were again ignited when Atheneus Eudecia came to live there. Jewish scholars of the Galilee allegedly wrote their brethren that the time of exile had passed, "for the Roman kings have ordained that our city Jerusalem will be restored to us." Certainly, the ban against visiting Jerusalem was revoked. It is noteworthy that in June, 1968, archeologists unearthed an oil lamp used by a Jewish pilgrim of the fourth or fifth century when he visited the southern wall. Byzantine documents of the fifth and sixth centuries further verify the fact that Jews ventured to live in sections of the city that were legally prohibited to them, and the authorities, it would appear, did not restrict them.

In 614, hoping to secure the same autonomy the Persian government had granted the Jews of Babylon, Jewish battalions in Jerusalem rebelled against Byzantine officials and made a pact with the invading forces. As a result, for a few months Jerusalem was again under Jewish administrative control. The Jews quickly rallied to rid the city of alien altars and to prepare the site for a third Temple. But they were betrayed by the Persians, and the Christian citizens strove to restrict the Jews once more.

A quarter of a century later, in 638, the city fell to invading Arabs from Arabia. Omar granted the Jews legal rights as non-

Islamic subjects obligated to pay special taxes. There is no reason to doubt the authenticity of the eleventh-century document from the Cairo Geniza, according to which the Jews showed Omar the Temple site on which he erected a mosque. Jewish academies returned to Jerusalem, world Jewry again turned to its scholars for instruction, and students came to the city to study. Donations and queries from various European congregations also flowed into Jerusalem. During the 433 years of Arab rule, however, Jerusalem never became the seat of Arab government. Throughout those centuries, the Jews of Jerusalem were overtaxed, subjected to the caprices of despotic rulers, and regularly beset by plague and drought. On many occasions they had to appeal for assistance from prosperous and influential kinsfolk in various Arab countries. In particular, the Jews of Fustat interceded on behalf of Jerusalem's Jews and offered substantial support.

In 1077 the Seljuk Turks conquered the city; it never returned to Arab rule except for the recent Jordanian control of the Old City prior to 1967. On July 15, 1099, the Crusaders occupied Jerusalem. They encountered Jewish defenders fighting alongside the Turks and Arabs. The Crusaders slaughtered the Jews, and those not massacred were sold as slaves in European markets. The Jews of Egypt and Italy ransomed many of the victims. In the final phase of the First Crusade, Baldwin I reenacted the edict forbidding Jews to reside in Jerusalem. But as in the past, practical considerations compelled the local authorities to grant Jewish families domiciliary rights. As a result, Jews inhabited Jerusalem throughout the duration of the Latin Kingdom. Without knights to defend the city, Latin Jerusalem fell to Saladin in 1187. As the Crusaders returned to Europe, Jews became convinced that the land of Israel would never yield itself permanently to any foreign power; hence they themselves felt moved to resettle it. Fresh waves of immigrants arrived in Jerusalem from France and Germany. But when the Mongols destroyed the city in the second half of the thirteenth century, many of the Jewish inhabitants fled and returned only during the Mamelukes' occupation of Jerusalem. For the next two centuries conditions in the city so deteriorated that by the middle of the fifteenth century, shortly before the expulsion of the Jews from Spain, not more than one hundred Jewish families may have been living there.

As a direct consequence of the expulsion, Jews from Spain comprised the major influx to Jerusalem. In 1516 the city fell to the Ottoman Turks, who constituted the ruling power for the next four hundred years. But while their administrators and officials were rapidly assimilated, their language never replaced Arabic as the vernacular of the country. This era is one of the richest in primary sources. The Turks conducted frequent censuses apparently the better to exact heavy taxes. One evil for which these tyrants are still remembered was the hydra of taxation, assessments, and special levies. Jewish documents from Jerusalem decry the resulting vicious circle. The oppressive taxes compelled the Jewish leaders to borrow money from Arab lenders at exorbitant rates. These loans exacerbated the situation by further burdening the community whose commercial and industrial resources were already seriously limited. The Jews were frequently threatened with eviction, imprisonment, and death. Such perils constantly induced Jewish rabbinic and lay leaders to dispatch emissaries (*sheliḥim*) or letters of appeal to arouse the various Jewish communities of North Africa, Europe, and Turkey to lend assistance and thereby forestall the immediate danger. Aid was generally forthcoming. Gradually special funds and levies were established for the maintenance and security of Jerusalem's Jewry and its educational and religious institutions. At the beginning of the eighteenth century, for example, upon learning of the atrocities committed by local officers against rabbis and Jewish leaders in Jerusalem, the Jews of Constantinople set up a permanent council to direct the political and economic affairs of Jerusalem.

From that era to fairly recent times, the Jewish community in Jerusalem was composed of four groups determined by their land of origin: Ashkenazi, of East European and Italian background; Sephardi, the majority of whom were descendants of refugees from Spain; Mug'abi from North Africa; and Mustarabs, or native Jews who had lived in the land for centuries. Throughout the hundreds of years of Ottoman rule, students and scholars flocked to Jerusalem. Each migration brought its own traditions and established its own institutions, thereby contributing to Jerusalem's character and growth. During the eighteenth century Ashkenazis were officially banned from the city, yet about fifty secretly remained. Consequently, when the brother-in-law of the Baal Shem Tov, the founder of Ḥasidism, arrived in Jerusalem, he had to masquerade as a Sephardi. Matters worsened to the point that in 1761 the local Jewish officials, not wishing to aggravate the situation, took steps to restrict the size of the Jewish community. These self-imposed ordinances were as ineffective as the official edicts and did not stop the steady, albeit small, flow of Jews to Jerusalem. Thus, neither ban prevented the followers of the Gaon of Vilna, the Perushim, from coming to live in Jerusalem and from making their specific contribution to the reconstituted Ashkenazi community.

As Turkey lost its prestige and power during the nineteenth century, foreign countries began demanding extraterritorial rights for their citizens living under Turkish rule. Henceforth, many Jews were protected by foreign consuls who viewed them as a potential method of limiting Turkey's expansion. The growth and modernization of Jerusalem were also aided by wealthy and distinguished Western Jews who visited Jerusalem, interested themselves in its welfare, and contributed toward the building of schools, hospitals, and residential suburbs. Most famous of these was Sir Moses Montefiore, who, among other things, made it possible for five hundred Jews to become gainfully employed in agriculture, and who also founded the new Jerusalem outside the Old City walls. In 1854, with a sum of sixty thousand dollars bequeathed by Judah Touro, an American, for the express purpose of building homes for Jerusalem's Jews, Montefiore, as executor, had the first complex of houses built south of the wall. By 1895 over one half of Jerusalem's Jews lived outside the wall. Needless to say, the latter demonstrated considerable courage in exposing themselves to the bands of thieves and bandits who roamed the area. It is interesting to note that all Turkish and Jewish statistics of this century indicate that by this time the Jews constituted a clear majority in Jerusalem. At the termination of Turkish rule, there were 47,400 Jews, 9,800 Moslems, and 16,400 Christians in the city.

During the British Mandate, Jerusalem served as the administrative center of the rapidly growing Jewish community of *Eretz Yisrael,* as well as of British officialdom. The new growth of Jerusalem was stifled as early as 1920 because of Arab opposition to the Jewish residents of both sectors of Jerusalem. For the next quarter of a century many Jerusalemites were harassed and murdered, while the mandatory power proved unable to prevent such attacks. Not a year passed without some kind of armed foray against the Jews.

Though the British Mandate terminated on May 18, 1948, the battles in Jerusalem started at the beginning of that year. In January, 1948, Arab marauders intensified their assaults upon the inhabitants of the city and engaged in guerrilla warfare along the entire road from Tel Aviv to Jerusalem. Three months later Jerusalem's main road was under siege and its pipeline cut. Its Jewish residents suffered bombardment and severe shortages of food and water. Daily rations consisted of fifty grams of bread and two liters of water. In April, seventy-seven doctors, nurses, and students were murdered on their way to the Hadassah Hospital on Mount Scopus. In the same month the Haganah Defense Forces successfully routed Iraqi troops who had invaded a southern section of the New City. The seventeen hundred Jewish residents of the Old City were isolated from the hundred thousand Jews of the New City. The latter were themselves isolated from the main Jewish segments of the country. When the State of Israel was established in May, 1948, Jerusalem became its capital, and on February 14, 1949, the first Israel Parliament convened there.

When the cease-fire became effective, the Old City and the road to Mount Scopus were held by the Arab Legion. However, Article 8, Paragraph 2 of the Israel-Jordan Armistice Agreements of 1949 specifically guaranteed "free movement of traffic on vital roads including the Bethlehem-Latrun-Jerusalem roads; resumption of the normal functioning of the cultural and humanitarian institutions on Mount Scopus and free access thereto; free access to the Holy Places and cultural institutions and use of the cemetery on the Mount of Olives . . ." With the exception of the clause concerning access to Mount Scopus, these provisions were not honored by Jordan, and the Jewish population was refused access to its most sacred shrines.

In the latter half of May, 1967, Jordan and Egypt signed a mutual defense pact, which placed the Jordanian Armed Forces under Egyptian Command. On June 5, in spite of a message from the Prime Minister of Israel guaranteeing no initiation of any action against Jordan, a full-scale attack on several sections of the New City was launched by the Arab Legion, and the U.N. Headquarters Building was captured. After a fierce battle which lasted for two days, the Old City was captured by the Israeli Forces, and Jerusalem was reunited.

Today more than two hundred thousand Jews, approximately sixty thousand Arabs, and six thousand persons of other origins live in Jerusalem.

Chapter One
EARLY HISTORY

For Jews the story of Jerusalem begins in the Bible.[1] Many epithets are used—"the place the Lord will choose," "Zion," "the City of David," "the dwelling place of the Most High," "the perfection of beauty," "the joy of the whole earth," "the city of the Great King"—but it is an actual city that is being described.

Despite their differing hypotheses as to the topography of Biblical Jerusalem, archeologists are in general agreement that it was located on the Southeast Hill known as Ophel. It is with this hill that the City of David is identified. Other details regarding the ancient city remain subject to controversy.

The narratives of the Pentateuch outline the story of Creation and the first generations of mankind, which in the Biblical view are preludes to the origins of the Israelites. This history is itself narrated in order to explain the unique covenantal relationship between God and His people that antedates the sojourn in Egypt and the release from bondage, which were divinely ordained as prerequisites for receiving the Torah and for settlement in the Land of Israel.

Deuteronomy introduces the idea of the centralization of Israelite cultic activities by repeatedly stressing "the place which

[1] The Hebrew Bible is divided into three major compilations: the Torah (Pentateuch), the Prophets, and the Writings. It contains materials spanning more than fifteen hundred years of Israelite history, from the pre-patriarchal era to the events just prior to the Maccabean revolt. The narratives, laws, poems, exhortations, proverbs, and prayers reflect the basic tenets and practices of Israelite ethical monotheism. Passages from the Pentateuch are taken from *The Torah* (1962), while all other Biblical passages are based upon *The Holy Scriptures* (1917). See Further Readings.

27

YHWH [2] will choose." Some scholars maintain that the site
alluded to is Jerusalem, although it is not mentioned specifically.
Deuteronomy stipulates that this site and its sanctuary are destined, once the Israelites are permanently settled on their land, to
be the exclusive center for all rites related to the worship of
YHWH.

The sacredness of the shrine is transferred to the city to the
extent that certain observances, although not performed within
the holy precincts, can be fulfilled only within the boundaries of
the chosen city. According to Deuteronomy, the Passover festival
can be solemnized only in Jerusalem, the seven days of the Feast
of Tabernacles are to be spent there, and there too the "first
fruits" are to be brought. "Three times a year—on the Feast of
Unleavened Bread, on the Feast of Weeks, and on the Feast of
Booths—all your males shall appear before the Lord your God in
the place that He will choose. They shall not appear before the
Lord empty-handed, but each with his own gift, according to the
blessing that the Lord your God has bestowed upon you." [3] That
city is also to house the court of highest appeal.

The Books of Joshua and Judges may be read as quasi-historical
accounts written with a marked theological approach. They recount the story of the Israelite conquest and settlement prior to the
period of David, the conqueror of Jerusalem. Throughout this
period, generally dated between the years 1220–1170 B.C.E., it
appears that Jerusalem remained a Jebusite city. "And as for the
Jebusites, the inhabitants of Jerusalem, the children of Judah
could not drive them out; but the Jebusites dwelt with the children
of Judah at Jerusalem, unto this day." [4] This is reconfirmed in
Judges 1:21.

[2] YHWH is the Tetragrammaton, consisting of the Hebrew letters *Yod
He Vav He,* and considered by rabbinic tradition to be the essential name
of God.
[3] Deut. 16:16–17.
[4] Josh. 15:63.

City of David
(1000–961 B.C.E.)

Sometime during the tenth century before the Common Era
Jerusalem became the City of David. David's story is the subject
of First Samuel. But it is in Second Samuel that Jerusalem begins
to play a central role.

> And the king [David] and his men went to Jerusalem against the
> Jebusites, the inhabitants of the land, who spoke unto David, say-
> ing: "Except you take away the blind and the lame, you shall not
> come in hither"; thinking, "David cannot come in hither." Never-
> theless David took the stronghold of Zion; that is the city of Da-
> vid. . . . And David dwelt in the stronghold, and called it the
> city of David. And David built round about from Millo and
> inward. . . . And Hiram, king of Tyre, sent messengers to David,
> and cedar-trees and carpenters, and masons: and they built David
> a house.[5]

David made Jerusalem the home of the Ark of the Lord.

> David went and brought up the ark of God from the house of
> Obed-Edom into the city of David with joy. When they that bore
> the ark of the Lord had gone six paces, he sacrificed an ox. And
> David danced before the Lord with all his might; and David was
> girded with a linen ephod. . . . They brought in the ark of the
> Lord, and set it in its place, in the midst of the tent that David
> had pitched for it; and David offered burnt-offerings and peace-
> offerings, he blessed the people in the name of the Lord of hosts.
> And he dealt among all the people, even among the whole multi-
> tude of Israel, both to men and women, to every one a cake of
> bread, and a cake made in a pan, and a sweet cake.[6]

When David planned to build a permanent temple for the Ark,
the prophet Nathan informed him of God's word: "When your
days are fulfilled and you shall sleep with your fathers, I will

[5] 5:6–12.
[6] *Ibid.* 6:12–19.

set up your seed after you, that shall proceed out of your body, and I shall establish his kingdom. He shall build a house for My name and I will establish the throne of his kingdom forever." [7]

Solomon and the Temple
(961–922 B.C.E.)

The Books of Kings and Chronicles contain elaborate details about the ensuing history of Jerusalem and the Kingdom of Judah. In the second half of the tenth century Solomon built the Temple. He ordered the timber from Hiram, king of Tyre, and paid him in cattle, wheat, and oil. To import and prepare the necessary materials, quarry the stone, and help in the construction, Solomon levied a corvee of thirty thousand men, who assisted the king's builders and Hiram's architects. A detailed description of the Temple and Solomon's palace is presented in First Kings (chaps. 6 and 7).

> Then Solomon assembled the elders of Israel, and all the heads of the tribes, the princes of the fathers' houses of the children of Israel, unto king Solomon in Jerusalem, to bring up the ark of the covenant of the Lord out of the city of David, which is Zion.[8]

And Solomon said:

> I have surely built You a house of habitation,
> A place for You to dwell in for ever.[9]

The Lord responded thus to Solomon:

> I have heard your prayer and your supplication that you made before Me; I have hallowed this house, which you have built, to put My name there forever. My eyes and My heart shall be there perpetually. And as for you, if you will walk before Me, as David your father walked . . . then I will establish the throne of your kingdom over Israel forever; . . . but if you shall turn away from

[7] *Ibid.* 7:12.
[8] 1 Kings 8:1.
[9] *Ibid.*, v. 13.

following Me . . . then will I cut off Israel out of the land which I have given them: and this house which I have hallowed for My name, will I cast out of My sight.[10]

The Kingdom Divided
(922–722 B.C.E.)

According to the author of First Kings, God soon became angry with Solomon because of the pagan temples he had built in Jerusalem for his foreign wives. It is very likely that the insurrection and eventual secession of the northern kingdom took place as a direct result of the heavy burdens imposed upon the citizenry for the maintenance of his luxurious palaces. Scholars fix the year 922 as the date of renunciation of the Davidic kingdom by the northern tribes.

> Wherefore the Lord said unto Solomon: . . . Howbeit I will not rend away all the kingdom; but I will give one tribe to your son, for David My servant's sake, and for Jerusalem's sake which I have chosen.[11]

About 918, Shishak, who founded the Twenty-second Dynasty in Egypt, led the Egyptian armies against the land and laid both Israel and Judah waste.

> And it came to pass in the fifth year of king Rehoboam, that Shishak king of Egypt came up against Jerusalem, and he took away the treasures of the house of the Lord, and the treasures of the king's house; he even took away all; and he took away all the shields of gold which Solomon had made. And king Rehoboam made in their stead shields of brass, and committed them to the hands of the guard, who kept the door of the king's house.[12]

Chronicles, composed during the early period of the Second Temple, idealizes the Davidic dynasty and its achievements. It

[10] *Ibid.* 9:3–7.
[11] *Ibid.* 11:11–13.
[12] *Ibid.* 14:25–27.

relates how Uzziah (783–742), who became king of Judah at the age of sixteen, "built towers in Jerusalem at the corner gate and at the valley gate, and at the Turning, and fortified them." [13]

Hezekiah (715–697), king of Judah, rebelled against Assyrian rule in 705. In preparation for a siege, "he made the pool, and the conduit, and brought water into the city." This is the Siloam tunnel, designed to bring the waters of the Gihon into the city. In 701 Sennacherib crushed the rebellion and reached Jerusalem.

> The king of Assyria sent Tartan and Rab-saris and Rab-shakeh from Lachish to king Hezekiah with a great army unto Jerusalem. And they went up and they came to Jerusalem. . . . And Rab-shakeh said unto them . . . If you say unto me: We trust in the Lord our God; is not that He, whose high places and whose altars Hezekiah has taken away, and has said to Judah and to Jerusalem: You shall worship before this altar in Jerusalem? [14]

Prophetic Warnings

Throughout this period, the prophets of Israel were predicting Zion's doom and simultaneously forecasting a more brilliant future for Jerusalem. The prophetic books are our record of what they said. The impending catastrophe is always viewed as the divinely ordained precursor of a portentous epoch, an age of resplendence for Jerusalem.

Amos was among the first of the prophets to warn the Israelites about events to come.

> The Lord roars from Zion,
> And makes His voice sound from Jerusalem;
> And the pastures of the shepherds shall mourn,
> The top of Carmel shall wither.[15]

But the prophet concludes with words of comfort.

> In that day I will raise up
> The tabernacle of David that is fallen,

[13] 2 Chron. 26:9.
[14] 2 Kings 18:17, 19, 22.
[15] Amos 1:2.

> And close up the breaches thereof,
> I will raise up his ruins,
> And I will build it as in the days of old.[16]

Isaiah, a contemporary of Hezekiah, was apparently a Jerusalemite, and in his prophecies the name of Jerusalem always precedes that of Judah. Jerusalem lies at the center of his concern.

> Your country is desolate, your cities are burned with fire;
> your land, strangers devour it in your presence, it is
> desolate as overthrown by floods.
> The daughter of Zion is left as a booth in a vineyard,
> as a lodge in a garden of cucumbers, as a besieged city.[17]

But he is also the herald of an immortal vision of peace in which Jerusalem will be a lodestar for the nations.

> It shall come to pass in the end of days,
> That the mountain of the Lord's house shall be
> established at the top of the mountains,
> And shall be exalted above the hills;
> All nations shall flow unto it.
> Many peoples shall go and say:
> "Come, and let us go up to the mountain of
> the Lord,
> To the house of the God of Jacob;
> And He will teach us of His ways,
> And we will walk in His paths."
> For out of Zion shall go forth Torah,
> And the word of the Lord from Jerusalem.
> He shall judge between the nations,
> And shall decide for many peoples;
> They shall beat their swords into plowshares,
> And their spears into pruning-hooks;
> Nation shall not lift up sword against nation,
> Neither shall they learn war any more.[18]

Jerusalem will also enjoy divine protection.

> The Lord will create over the whole habitation of Mount Zion,
> and over her assemblies, a cloud and smoke by day, and the shining

[16] *Ibid.* 9:11.
[17] Isa. 1:7–8
[18] *Ibid.* 2:2–4.

of a flaming fire by night; for over all the glory shall be a canopy. And there shall be a pavilion for a shadow in the day-time from the heat and for a refuge and for a covert from storm and from rain.[19]

> For thus says the Lord unto me:
> Like as the lion, or the young lion growling over his prey,
> Though a multitude of shepherds be called forth against him
> Will not be dismayed at their voice,
> Nor abase himself at their noise,
> So will the Lord of hosts come down
> To fight upon Mount Zion, and upon the hill thereof.
> As birds hovering,
> So will the Lord of hosts protect Jerusalem;
> He will deliver it as He protects it,
> He will protect it as He passes over.[20]

Micah, Isaiah's contemporary, followed the usual prophetic pattern. First he foresaw doom and calamity.

> For this will I wail and howl,
> I will go stripped and naked;
> I will make a wailing like the jackals,
> And a mourning like the ostriches.
> For her wound is incurable,
> For it is come unto Judah;
> It reaches unto the gate of my people, unto Jerusalem.[21]

Then he comforted his people with a vision of peace similar to that of Isaiah.

> I will make her that halted a remnant,
> And her that was cast far off a mighty nation;
> And the Lord shall reign over them in Mount Zion
>   from thenceforth even for ever.[22]

By 622, Josiah's reforms had been put into effect. The "Book of the Torah," generally identified with Deuteronomy, had been found and the centralization of the cult initiated. We read of the

[19] *Ibid*. 4:5–6.
[20] *Ibid*. 31:4–5.
[21] Mic. 1:8–9.
[22] *Ibid*. 4:7.

purge of pagan altars, the rededication ceremonies, and the celebration of Passover held in Jerusalem that year.

The king sent, and they gathered unto him all the elders of
Judah and of Jerusalem. The king went up to the house of the
Lord, and all the men of Judah and all the inhabitants of Jerusalem with him, and the priests and the prophets, and all the
people, both lowly and great. He read in their ears all the
words of the book of the covenant which was found in the house
of the Lord. The king stood on the platform and made a
covenant before the Lord, to walk after the Lord, and to keep
His commandments, His testimonies, and His statutes, with all
his heart, and all his soul, to confirm the words of this covenant
that were written in this book; and all the people stood to the
covenant. The king commanded Hilkiah, the high priest, and the
priests of the second order and the keepers of the door to bring
forth out of the temple of the Lord all the vessels that were made
for Baal, and for the Asherah, and for all the host of heaven; and
he burned them outside of Jerusalem in the fields of Kidron.[23]

Although the prophecies of Zephaniah are not directly linked
to any historical events, they hint at events following the death of
Assurbanipal in 633, which signaled the beginning of the collapse
of the Assyrian Empire.

> Sing, O daughter of Zion,
> Shout, O Israel;
> Be glad and rejoice with all your heart,
> O daughter of Jerusalem.
> The Lord has taken away your judgments,
> He has cast out your enemy . . .
> In that day it shall be said to Jerusalem;
> "Fear not,
> O Zion, let not your hands be slack.
> The Lord your God is in your midst,
> A Mighty One who will save;
> He will rejoice over you with joy,
> He will be silent in His love,
> He will make you glad with singing." [24]

[23] 2 Kings 23:1–4.
[24] Zeph. 3:14–17.

Jeremiah commenced his prophecies in the thirteenth year of Josiah's reign (*ca.* 627) and warned his people throughout the four decades preceding the destruction of the Temple.

Return, O backsliding children, says the Lord; for I am a lord unto you; I will take you one of a city, and two of a family, and I will bring you to Zion; and I will give you shepherds according to My heart, who shall feed you with knowledge and understanding. . . . At that time they shall call Jerusalem The throne of the Lord; and all the nations shall be gathered unto it, to the name of the Lord, to Jerusalem; neither shall they walk any more after the stubbornness of their evil heart.[25]

Put yourselves under cover, children of Benjamin,
Away from the midst of Jerusalem,
And blow the horn in Tekoa,
And set up a signal on Beth-cherem;
For evil looks forth from the north,
And a great destruction.
The comely and delicate one,
The daughter of Zion, will I cut off.
Shepherds with their flocks come unto her;
They pitch their tents against her round about . . .

"Prepare war against her;
Arise, let us go up at noon!"
"Woe unto us! for the day declines,
For the shadows of the evening are stretched out!"
"Arise and let us go up by night,
And let us destroy her palaces."

For thus has the Lord of hosts said:
Hew down her trees,
And cast up a mound against Jerusalem;
This is the city to be punished;
Everywhere there is oppression in her midst. . . .
Be corrected, O Jerusalem,
Lest My soul be alienated from you,
Lest I make you desolate,
A land not inhabited.[26]

[25] Jer. 3:14–17.
[26] *Ibid.* 6:1–8.

Behold, the days are coming . . . when I will cause to cease from the cities of Judah and from the streets of Jerusalem, the voice of mirth and the voice of gladness, the voice of the bridegroom and the voice of the bride; for the land shall be desolate.[27]

Destruction of Jerusalem (587 B.C.E)
and Exile

In 597, ten years after the destruction of Jerusalem, King Jehoiachin was exiled, as described in Second Kings.

At that time the servants of Nebuchadnezzar king of Babylon came up to Jerusalem and the city was besieged. And Nebuchadnezzar king of Babylon came unto the city while his servants were besieging it. Jehoiachin the king of Judah went out to the king of Babylon, he, and his mother, and his servants, and his princes, and his officers; and the king of Babylon took him in the eighth year of his reign. He carried out thence all the treasures of the house of the Lord, and the treasures of the king's house, and cut in pieces all the vessels of gold which Solomon king of Israel had made in the Temple of the Lord, as the Lord had said. And he carried away all Jerusalem, and all the princes, and all the mighty men of valor, even ten thousand captives, and all the craftsmen and the smiths; none remained save the poorest sort of the people of the land. He carried away Jehoiachin to Babylon; and the king's mother, and the king's wives, and his officers, and the chief men of the land, carried he into captivity from Jerusalem to Babylon. And seven thousand men of might, and a thousand craftsmen and smiths, all of them strong and apt for war, even them the king of Babylon brought captive to Babylon.[28]

The events of 587 are described in Second Kings.

Zedekiah rebelled against the king of Babylon. And it came to pass in the ninth year of his reign, in the tenth month, in the tenth day of the month, that Nebuchadnezzar king of Babylon

27 *Ibid.* 7:32–34.
28 24:10–16.

came, he and all his army, against Jerusalem, and encamped against it; and they built forts against it round about. So the city was besieged unto the eleventh year of king Zedekiah. On the ninth day of the [fourth] month the famine was sore in the city, so that there was no bread for the people of the land. Then a breach was made in the city, and all the men of war [fled] by night by the way of the gate between the two walls, which was by the king's garden—now the Chaldeans were against the city round about—and the king went by way of the Arabah. But the army of the Chaldeans pursued after the king, and overtook him in the plains of Jericho; and all his army was scattered from him. Then they took the king, and carried him up unto the king of Babylon to Riblah; and they gave judgment upon him. And they slew the sons of Zedekiah before his eyes, and put out the eyes of Zedekiah, and bound him in fetters, and carried him to Babylon.

Now, in the fifth month, on the seventh day of the month, which was the nineteenth year of king Nebuchadnezzar, king of Babylon, came Nebuzaradan the captain of the guard, a servant of the king of Babylon, to Jerusalem. And he burned the house of the Lord, and the king's house; and all the houses of Jerusalem, even every great man's house, burnt he with fire. And all the army of the Chaldeans, that were with the captain of the guard, broke down the walls of Jerusalem round about. And the residue of the people that were left in the city, and those that fell away, that fell to the king of Babylon, and the residue of the multitude, did Nebuzaradan the captain of the guard carry away captive. But the captain of the guard left of the poorest of the land to be vinedressers and husbandmen.

And the pillars of brass that were in the house of the Lord, and the bases and the brazen sea that were in the house of the Lord, did the Chaldeans break in pieces, and carried the brass of them to Babylon. And the pots, and the shovels, and the snuffers, and the pans, and all the vessels of brass wherewith they ministered, took they away.[29]

The theme of Lamentations is the devastation of Jerusalem and the pillage of the First Temple. Tradition attributes it to the prophet Jeremiah. Most modern scholars, while not identifying its author or authors with any known figure, agree that it was composed soon

[29] 25:1–14.

after the fall of Jerusalem. The Temple has been defiled, though no mention is made of its destruction. The wall around the city still stands, though its gates "are desolate" and have "sunk to the ground." Jerusalem, still inhabited, is blighted and vandalized. Its residents thirst for water, vainly seek food, and fear the enemy.

In five tragic chapters, the first four of which are alphabetic acrostics, the poet eulogizes Jerusalem in dirge rhythms as he recalls its past grandeur. Since this threnody was chanted annually on the Fast of the Ninth of Av, the similes, hyperboles, metonymies, and personifications pertaining to Jerusalem became the standard literary materials for all future composers of *kinnot* (dirges), regardless of subject.

The city is personified as an inconsolable widow, a forsaken or deceived lover, a betrayed friend, a remorseful sinner, one whom God has abandoned and delivered to His adversaries. In a refrain which was to be repeated throughout Jewish literature, the author confesses his inability to find words to express the horrors of the holocaust.

> What shall I take to witness for you? What shall I liken to you,
> O daughter of Jerusalem? . . .
> All that pass by clap
> their hands at you;
> They hiss and wag their heads
> At the daughter of Jerusalem:
> "Is this the city that men called
> The perfection of beauty,
> The joy of the whole earth?" [30]

> How does the city sit solitary,
> That was full of people!
> How is she become as a widow!
> She that was great among the nations,
> And princess among the provinces,
> How is she become tributary!
> She weeps sore in the night,
> And her tears are on her cheeks;
> She has none to comfort her

[30] Lam. 2:13–15.

> Among all her lovers;
> All her friends have dealt treacherously with her,
> They have become her enemies . . .
> The roads of Zion do mourn,
> Because none come to the solemn assembly:
> All her gates are desolate,
> Her priests sigh;
> Her maidens are afflicted,
> And she herself is in bitterness.[31]

In the manner of all the great prophets, Jeremiah, himself still a prisoner, after confronting his people with the realities of their tragic situation, applied himself to the task of renewing their hope with visions of redemption.

> And this city shall be to Me for a name of joy, for a praise and for a glory, before all the nations of the earth which shall hear all the good that I do unto them. . . . Thus says the Lord: Yet again there shall be heard in this place, whereof you say: It is waste, without man and without beast, even in the cities of Judah, and in the streets of Jerusalem, that are desolate, without man and without inhabitant and without beast, the voice of joy and the voice of gladness, the voice of the bridegroom and the voice of the bride, the voice of them that say: "Give thanks to the Lord of hosts, for the Lord is good, for His mercy endures for ever," even of them that bring offerings of thanksgiving into the house of the Lord. For I will cause the captivity of the land to return as at the first, says the Lord . . .
>> In those days shall Judah be saved,
>> And Jerusalem shall dwell safely;
>> And this is the name whereby she shall be called,
>> The Lord is our righteousness.[32]

Ezekiel began to prophecy in 592, and the latest of his pronouncements is dated 570 by scholars. Until the destruction of the Temple he forecast doom and ruin for Jerusalem. After its destruction, the mood changes and he comforts the people with prophecies of Jerusalem's restoration under a Davidic king. Ap-

---

[31] *Ibid.*, 1:1–4.
[32] Jer. 33:9–16.

parently Ezekiel was deported as part of the "exile of Jehoiachin" in 597, and all his prophecies were delivered to the exiled Jewish community in Babylon. Exiled with King Jehoiachin, he addresses his brethren in the first exile in Jewish history and senses that his compatriots feel themselves a severed branch of the still extant Jerusalem community. The dilemma they faced concerned their fate should Jerusalem fall. Ezekiel informs them that Jerusalem must be destroyed, but its restoration will depend on their repentance and eventual return to the city.

> You, son of man, take a tile, and lay it before you, and trace upon it the city of Jerusalem; and lay siege against it, and build forts against it, and cast up a mound against it; set camps also against it, and set battering rams against it round about. . . . This shall be a sign to the house of Israel. . . . Moreover, He said to me: "Son of man, behold, I will break the staff of bread in Jerusalem, and they shall eat bread by weight, and with anxiety; and they shall drink water by measure, and with apprehension; that they may want bread and water, and be appalled one with the other, and pine away in their iniquity." [33]

Return and Restoration
(537 B.C.E.)

After Cyrus, founder of a new Persian empire, conquered the Babylonians about 537, he invited the Jews to return to Judah and rebuild their Temple in Jerusalem. The text of his proclamation and the description of the "return" were recorded in the Book of Ezra, the scribe who came from Babylon to help rebuild Jerusalem.

> Thus says Cyrus king of Persia: All the kingdoms of the earth has the Lord, the God of heaven, given me; and He has charged me to build Him a house in Jerusalem which is in Judah. Whoever there is among you of all His people—his God be with him—let him

---

[33] Ezek. 4. The later chapters of Ezekiel contain elaborate and fantastic visions of the future temple and city of Jerusalem.

go up to Jerusalem, which is in Judah, and build the house of the Lord, the God of Israel, He is the God who is in Jerusalem. But whosoever remains, in any place where he lives, let the men of his place help him with silver, and gold, and with goods, and with beasts, beside the freewill offering for the house of God which is in Jerusalem.[34]

According to Ezra, fifty thousand Jews returned to Jerusalem together with their leaders. The exact year of their arrival is unknown, but it is commonly fixed at a year or two following the proclamation of Cyrus.

When the seventh month [Tishri] was come, and the children of Israel were in the cities, the people gathered themselves together as one man to Jerusalem. Then stood up Jeshua, the son of Jozadak, and his brethren the priests, and Zerubbabel son of Shealtiel, and his brethren, and built the altar of the God of Israel, to offer burnt-offerings thereon, as it is written in the Torah of Moses, the man of God.[35]

Deutero-Isaiah, the leading prophet of the restoration period, predicted a glorious future to comfort the returnees, many of whom still remembered Jerusalem's past and despaired of the present. He delivered his consolations in Babylonia. His prophecies, comprising Chapters 40–66 of the Book of Isaiah, span the years of the ascent of Cyrus in 550 to approximately 530 B.C.E. Curiously, however, Deutero-Isaiah makes no mention of the return of the exiles.

> Comfort you, comfort you, My people,
> Says your God.
> Bid Jerusalem take heart,
> And proclaim unto her,
> That her time of service is accomplished,
> That her guilt is paid off;
> That she has received from the Lord's hand
> Double for all her sins. . . .
>
> O you who bring good tidings to Zion,
> Go up to the high mountain;

[34] 1:2–4; see also 6:3–5.
[35] 3:1–2.

O you who announce good tidings to Jerusalem,
Lift up your voice with strength;
Lift it up, be not afraid;
Say to the cities of Judah:
"Behold your God!"
Behold, the Lord God will come as a Mighty One,
And His arm will rule for Him,
Behold, His reward is with Him,
And His recompense before Him.[36]

Awake, awake, put on your glory, O Zion,
Put on your beautiful garments,
O Jerusalem, the holy city;
For henceforth there shall no more come into you
The uncircumcised and the unclean.
Shake yourself from the dust;
Arise, and sit down, O Jerusalem;
Loosen yourself from the bands of your neck
O captive daughter of Zion. . . .

Break forth into joy, sing together,
Waste places of Jerusalem;
For the Lord has comforted His people,
He has redeemed Jerusalem.[37]

For Zion's sake I will not hold My peace;
And for Jerusalem's sake I will not rest,
Until her triumph go forth as brightness,
And her victory as a burning torch. . . .

You shall be a crown of beauty in the hand of the Lord.
And a royal diadem in the open hand of your God.
You shall no more be called Forsaken,
Neither shall your land any more be called Desolate
But you shall be called, My delight is in her,
And your land, Espoused.
For the Lord delights in you,
And your land shall be espoused.
For as a young man espouses a virgin,
So shall your sons espouse you;

[36] 40:1–10.
[37] 52:1–9.

And as the bridegroom rejoices over the bride,
So shall your God rejoice over you.

I have set watchmen
Upon your walls, O Jerusalem,
They shall never hold their peace,
Day nor night;
"You that are the Lord's remembrancers
Take no rest,
And give Him no rest,
Till He establish
And till He make Jerusalem
A praise in the earth." [38]

Behold, I create Jerusalem a rejoicing,
And her people a joy.
I will rejoice in Jerusalem,
And joy in My people;
The voice of weeping shall be no more heard in her,
Nor the voice of crying . . .
And they shall build houses, and inhabit them;
And they shall plant vineyards, and eat their fruit.[39]

Rejoice with Jerusalem,
And be glad with her, all who love her;
Rejoice for joy with her
All who mourn for her. . . .
Behold, I will extend peace to her like a river . . .
As one whom his mother comforts,
So I will comfort you;
And you shall be comforted in Jerusalem.[40]

[38] 62:1–7.
[39] 65:18–21.
[40] 66:10–13.

Building the Second Temple
(537–515 B.C.E.)

In Iyar of the second year after the return (537/536), under the leadership of Zerubbabel and Jeshua, who had hired craftsmen and ordered materials for the rebuilding of the Temple, the people again convened in Jerusalem to celebrate the laying of its foundation.

> When the builders laid the foundation of the Temple of the Lord, they set the priests in their apparel with trumpets and the Levites, the sons of Asaph with cymbals, to praise the Lord, according to the direction of David king of Israel. They sang one to another, praised and thanked the Lord: "for He is good, for His mercy endures forever toward Israel." The people shouted with a great shout when they praised the Lord, because the foundation of the house of the Lord was laid. But many of the priests and Levites and heads of fathers' houses, the old men that had seen the former Temple standing on its foundation, wept loudly, when they saw this Temple, whereas many shouted for joy; so that the people could not discern the noise of the shout of joy from the noise of the weeping of the people; for the people shouted so loudly that the noise was heard afar off.[41]

Owing to external factors, suspicious neighbors, and the controversies with the Samaritans, the construction of the Temple was halted. It seems that Cyrus' proclamation referred only to the Temple but did not permit the rebuilding of the city and its walls. Nevertheless, during the reign of Cambyses (530–522) the returnees decided to repair the walls and rebuild the city's houses in order to protect themselves against invaders and marauders. This was reported by Rehum, the commander, and Jerusalem was called rebellious and seditious. Work was halted until the second year of Darius' reign.

[41] Ezra 3:10–13.

The two chapters of the Book of Haggai consist of four prophecies dated during the second year of the reign of Darius I (520).

Thus says the Lord of hosts, "This people say: the time is not come . . . for the Lord's house to be built." Then came the word of the Lord by Haggai the prophet saying: "Is it a time for you yourselves to dwell in your panelled houses, while this house lies desolate?" [42]

Who is left among you that saw this house in its former glory? and how do you see it now? is not this one as nothing in your eyes? Yet now be strong, Zerubbabel, says the Lord, and be strong, O Joshua, son of Jehozadak, the High Priest; and be strong, all you people of the land, says the Lord, and work; for I am with you, says the Lord of hosts. . . . Mine is the silver, and Mine the gold . . . The glory of this latter house shall be greater than that of the former, says the Lord of hosts; and in this place will I give peace.[43]

Zechariah began his prophecies about two months after Haggai. He was present at the celebrations for the laying of the foundation stone. The Book of Zechariah refers to events from the second to the fourth year of Darius' reign (520–518).

Thus says the Lord of hosts: I am zealous for Jerusalem and for Zion with great zealousness; and I am very sorely displeased with the nations that are at ease; for I was but a little displeased, and they helped for evil. Therefore thus says the Lord: I return to Jerusalem with compassion; My house shall be built in it, says the Lord of hosts, and a line shall be stretched forth over Jerusalem. Again, proclaim, saying: Thus says the Lord of hosts: My cities shall again overflow with prosperity, and the Lord shall yet comfort Zion, and shall yet choose Jerusalem.[44]

And I lifted up my eyes, and saw, and behold a man with a measuring line in his hand. Then I asked: "Where are you going?" And he said to me: "To measure Jerusalem, to see what is its breadth and what is its length." And, behold, the angel that spoke with me went forth, and another angel went out to meet him, and

[42] 1:2–4.
[43] 2:3–9.
[44] 1:14–17.

said unto him: "Run, speak to this young man, saying: Jerusalem shall be inhabited without walls, for the multitude of men and cattle therein. For I, says the Lord, will be unto her a wall of fire round about, and I will be the glory in the midst of her." . . .

"Sing and rejoice O daughter of Zion; for, lo, I come, and I will dwell in your midst, says the Lord. And many nations shall join themselves to the Lord on that day, and shall be My people, and I will dwell in your midst;" and you shall know that the Lord of hosts has sent me to you. And the Lord shall inherit Judah as His portion in the holy land, and shall choose Jerusalem again.[45]

And the word of the Lord of hosts came, saying: "Thus says the Lord of hosts: I am zealous for Zion with great zealousness, and I am zealous for her with great fury.

Thus says the Lord: I return unto Zion, and will dwell in the midst of Jerusalem; and Jerusalem shall be called The city of truth; and the mountain of the Lord of hosts The holy mountain.

Thus says the Lord of hosts: There shall yet old men and old women sit in the broad places of Jerusalem, every man with his staff in his hand for very age. And the broad places of the city shall be full of boys and girls playing in the broad places thereof. . . .

Thus says the Lord of hosts: Behold, I will save My people from the east country, and from the west country; and I will bring them, and they shall dwell in the midst of Jerusalem; and they shall be My people, and I will be their God, in truth and in righteousness.[46]

Nehemiah and Ezra
(*ca.* 440 B.C.E.)

There is a gap of almost a century in the Biblical sources. Scholars are still debating the date of Ezra's arrival (458 B.C.E. or 433 B.C.E.) and whether Ezra and Nehemiah ever met. The Books of Ezra and Nehemiah describe the rebuilding of the Temple and the

[45] 2:5–16.
[46] 8:1–8.

pressures and strains experienced by the Jewish returnees in Jerusalem during the age of restoration.

When the news reached Nehemiah of Jerusalem's dismal condition, he was dispatched to the city to serve as governor. He immediately set out to rebuild the walls.

> Then said I to them: "You see the evil case that we are in, how Jerusalem lies waste, and the gates thereof are burned with fire; come and let us build up the wall of Jerusalem, that we be no more a reproach." . . . And they said: "Let us rise up and build." So they strengthened their hands for the good work.[47]

> It came to pass, when our enemies heard that it [their plan] was known unto us, and God had brought their counsel to nought, that we returned all of us to the wall, every one to his work. And it came to pass from that time forth, that half my servants worked, while half of them held the spears, the shields, and the bows, and the coats of mail. . . . They that built the wall and they that bore burdens were heavy laden, every one with one of his hands carried on the work, and with the other held his weapon; and the builders, every one had his sword girded by his side, and so they built.[48]

After conquest by Alexander the Great, Jerusalem came under the rule of the Ptolemies. A detailed description, particularly of the Second Temple, appears in a letter written by an officer at the court of Ptolemy Philadelphus (285–247 B.C.E.).

> When we arrived in the land of the Jews we saw the city situated in the middle of the whole of Judea on the top of a mountain of considerable altitude. On the summit the Temple had been built in all its splendor. It was surrounded by three walls more than seventy cubits high and in length and breadth corresponding to the structure of the edifice. All the buildings were characterized by a magnificence and costliness quite unprecedented. It was obvious that no expense had been spared on the door and the fastenings, which connected it with the door-posts, and the stability of the lintel. . . .

> The Temple faces the east and its back is toward the west. The whole of the floor is paved with stones and slopes down to the

47 Neh. 2:17–18.
48 *Ibid.* 4:9–11.

appointed places, that water may be conveyed to wash away the blood from the sacrifices, for many thousand beasts are sacrificed there on the feast days. And there is an inexhaustible supply of water, because an abundant natural spring gushes up from within the Temple area. There are moreover wonderful and indescribable cisterns underground, as they pointed out to me, at a distance of five furlongs all round the site of the Temple, and each of them has countless pipes so that the different streams converge together. . . .

The ministration of the priests is in every way unsurpassed both for its physical endurance and for its orderly and silent service. For they all work spontaneously, though it entails much painful exertion, and each one has a special task allotted to him. The service is carried on without interruption—some provide the wood, others the oil, others the fine wheat flour, others the spices; others again bring the pieces of flesh for the burnt offering, exhibiting a wonderful degree of strength. . . . Everything is carried out with reverence and in a way worthy of the great God.

We were greatly astonished, when we saw Eleazar engaged in the ministration, at the mode of his dress, and the majesty of his appearance, which was revealed in the robe which he wore and the precious stones upon his person. There were golden bells upon the garment which reached down to his feet, giving forth a peculiar kind of melody, and on both sides of them there were pomegranates with variegated flowers of a wonderful hue. He was girded with a girdle of conspicuous beauty woven in the most beautiful colors. On his breast he wore the oracle of God, as it is called, on which twelve stones, of different kinds, were inset, fastened together with gold, containing the names of the leaders of the tribes, according to their original order, each one flashing forth in an indescribable way its own particular color. On his head he wore a tiara, as it is called, and upon this in the middle of his forehead an inimitable turban, the royal diadem full of glory with the name of God inscribed in sacred letters on a plate of gold. . . . having been judged worthy to wear these emblems in the ministrations. Their appearance created such awe and confusion of mind as to make one feel that one had come into the presence of a man who belonged to a different world. . . .

But in order that we might gain complete information, we ascended to the summit of the neighboring citadel and looked around us. It is situated in a very lofty spot, and is fortified with many towers, which have been built up to the very top of immense stones, with the object, as we were informed, of guarding the Temple precincts, so that if there were an attack, or an insurrection or an onslaught of the enemy, no one would be able to force an entrance within the walls that surround the Temple. On the towers of the citadel engines of war were placed and different kinds of machines, and the position was much higher than the circle of walls which I have mentioned. . . .

The size of the city is of moderate dimensions. It is about forty furlongs in circumference, as far as one could conjecture. It has its towers arranged in the shape of a theater, with thoroughfares leading between them. Now the cross roads of the lower towers are visible but those of the upper towers are more frequented. For the ground ascends, since the city is built upon a mountain. There are steps too which lead up to the cross roads, and some people are always going up, and others down and they keep as far apart from each other as possible on the road because of those who are bound by the rules of purity, lest they should touch anything which is unlawful. It was not without reason that the original founders of the city built it in due proportions, for they possessed clear insight with regard to what was required. For the country is extensive and beautiful.[49]

The Temple Plundered
(169 B.C.E.)

A century or so later, the Seleucids took over the rule of Jerusalem. After conquering Egypt, Antiochus, a Seleucid king, entered Jerusalem with a mighty force in 169 B.C.E., as is related in the First Book of Maccabees.

[49] "Letter of Aristeas," in R. H. Charles, ed., *Apocrypha and Pseudepigrapha of the Old Testament* (Oxford: Clarendon Press, 1913), 2:103–5. The date of composition is a subject of controversy among scholars, but several hold it to be of Maccabean origin.

In his arrogance he went into the sanctuary and took the golden altar, the candelabrum and all its vessels, the table for the show-bread, the cups, bowls, golden censers, curtains and crowns. And he stripped the gold ornamentation from the front of the temple, pillaged the silver and gold, and the choice dishes, and took the hidden treasures which he found. Having plundered everything, he made a great massacre, and returned triumphant to his own land. . . .

Two years later the king sent an officer to collect tribute from the cities of Judah, and he entered Jerusalem with a strong force. He spoke to them craftily so that they trusted him. Then suddenly he fell upon the city and smote it grievously and destroyed many of the people in Israel. He plundered the city, burned it down; and tore down its houses and the walls around it. They took the women and children captive and seized the cattle. Then they fortified the City of David with a great, strong wall, with strong towers, and it became their citadel. They placed sinful heathens there, who did not obey the Torah, and they entrenched themselves there. They stored up weapons and provisions, and they collected the spoils of Jerusalem there. And it became a sore threat, for it proved a place of ambush against the sanctuary and a constant evil adversary to Israel. They shed innocent blood all about the sanctuary, they defiled the sanctuary proper. The inhabitants of Jerusalem fled because of them. She became a place of strangers. . . .

Then the king sent word by messengers to Jerusalem and the towns of Judah ordering the practice of customs foreign to the land, forbidding the burnt offerings and the sacrifices and the drink offerings in the sanctuary, and commanding them to break the sabbaths . . . to build altars and sacrifice swine and other unclean animals, to leave their sons uncircumcised and make themselves abominable by means of everything that was unclean and profane, so that they might forget the Torah, and alter all the ordinances. And anyone who disobeyed the king's word should die.[50]

[50] Chap. 1.

Revolt of the Maccabees
(167–141 B.C.E.)

The revolt was led by Mattathias of Modin and his sons. After the death of Mattathias, the leadership fell to his son Judah (166–160), who waged a victorious campaign and was able to purify and rededicate the Temple (164 B.C.E.)

The whole army gathered and went up to Mount Zion. They found the sanctuary laid desolate, the altar profaned, the doors burned, and the weeds growing in the courts as they do in a forest or on some mountain, and the priests' quarters torn down. They rent their clothes, made great lamentation, covered themselves with ashes, and fell on their faces to the ground, and they blew solemn blasts on the trumpets, and cried out to heaven. Then Judah appointed men to fight the garrison in the citadel, until he could purify the sanctuary. And he chose pious priests who delighted in the Torah, and they cleansed the sanctuary, and carried out the defiled stones to an unclean place. And they took counsel what to do with the altar of burnt offerings which had been profaned. It seemed best to pull it down, lest it should be a reproach for them, because the heathen had defiled it. So they pulled it down, and laid the stones in a suitable place on the Temple mount, until a prophet should come and decide what was to be done with them. Then they took whole stones according to the Torah, and built a new altar like the previous one. They restored the sanctuary and the interior of the Temple, and consecrated the courts. They made new sacred vessels, and they brought into the Temple the candelabrum, and the altar for incense, and the table for showbread. Then they burned incense on the altar, and lighted the lights on the candelabrum to give light in the Temple. They set loaves on the table and hung up the curtains, and finished all the work they had undertaken.

They arose early on the twenty-fifth day af the ninth month, that is, the month of Kislev, in the one hundred and forty-eighth year (164/163) and offered sacrifice according to the Torah upon the new altar of burnt offering which they had made. At the corresponding time and on the day the heathen had profaned it, it was rededicated with songs, harps, lutes, and cymbals. All the people bowed and praised God who had prospered them. They celebrated the rededication of the altar for eight days and offered a sacrifice of deliverance and thanksgiving. . . . Judah and his brothers and all the people of Israel decreed that the days of rededication of the altar should be observed at their proper time, every year, for eight days beginning with the twenty-fifth day of the month of Kislev with gladness and joy.[51]

Destruction of the Second Temple
(70 C.E.)

After the capture of Jerusalem by Pompey in 63 B.C.E., the Romans held sway for four centuries. The Great Revolt, when the Jews resisted the Romans (66–70 C.E.) valiantly but in vain, and the ensuing fall of Jerusalem and the destruction of the Second Temple are documented by the historian Josephus.

Josephus was born (*ca.* 37 or 38 C.E.) in Jerusalem, where he lived and studied during his early years. Shortly after Josephus returned from a mission to Rome, the Jewish revolt against the Romans began, and the Sanhedrin appointed him governor in charge of the defense of Galilee. In May, 67, Josephus and his troops were besieged by Vespasian; they capitulated in July. From this point on, there is a suspicion of treachery. Vespasian granted Josephus his freedom, and in gratitude Josephus adopted Vespasian's family name "Flavius." Josephus returned to Jerusalem as part of Titus' retinue and attempted to persuade the Jews to surrender. Ultimately he was honored with Roman citizenship and an annual pension. Josephus' works include *The Wars of the Jews, The Antiquities of the Jews, Autobiography,* and *Against Apion.* In spite of the author's biases, the volumes that deal with Josephus' own period are important sources for our knowledge of events during those decades.

[51] *Ibid.,* Chap. 4.

In *The Wars of the Jews* at the point when Titus' legions pitch their tents at Jerusalem's gates and prepare for the attack, Josephus interrupts his narrative to describe the city.

The city was fortified by three walls, except where it was enclosed by impassable ravines, a single rampart there sufficing. It was built, in portions facing each other, on two hills separated by a central valley, in which the tiers of houses ended.

Of these hills that on which the upper city lay was far higher and had a straighter ridge than the other; consequently, owing to its strength it was called by King David—the father of Solomon, the first builder of the Temple—the Stronghold, but we called it the upper Agora. The second hill, which bore the name of Acra and supported the lower city, was a hog's back.

Opposite this was a third hill, by nature lower than Acra, and once divided from it by another broad ravine. Afterwards, however, the Hasmonaeans, during the period of their reign, both filled up the ravine, with the object of uniting the city to the Temple, and also reduced the elevation of Acra by leveling its summit, in order that it might not block the view of the Temple. The Valley of the Cheesemakers, as the ravine was called, . . . extends down to Siloam; for so we called that fountain of sweet and abundant water. On the exterior the two hills on which the city stood were encompassed by deep ravines, and the precipitous cliffs on either side of it rendered the town nowhere accessible. . . .

Above the wall, however, rose towers, twenty cubits broad and twenty high, square and solid as the wall itself, and in the joining and beauty of the stones in no wise inferior to a temple. Over this solid masonry, twenty cubits in altitude were magnificent apartments, and above these, upper chambers and cisterns to receive the rain-water, each tower having broad spiral staircases. Of such towers the third wall had ninety, disposed at intervals of two hundred cubits; the line of the middle wall was broken by fourteen towers, that of the old wall by sixty. The whole circumference of the city was thirty-three furlongs. . . .

Adjoining and on the inner side of these towers, which lay to the north of it, was the king's palace, baffling all description: indeed, in extravagance and equipment no building surpassed it. It was completely enclosed within a wall of thirty cubits high, broken at equal distances by ornamental towers, and contained immense banqueting-halls, and bed-chambers for a hundred guests. The interior fittings are indescribable—the variety of the stones (for species rare in every other country were here collected in abundance), ceilings wonderful both for the length of the beams and the splendor of their surface decoration, the host of apartments with their infinite varieties of design, all amply furnished, while most of the objects in each of them were of silver or gold. All around were many circular cloisters, leading one into another, the columns in each being different, and their open courts all of green-sward; there were groves of various trees intersected by long walks, which were bordered by deep canals, and ponds everywhere studded with bronze figures, through which the water was discharged, and around the streams were numerous cots for tame pigeons. However, it is impossible adequately to delineate the palace, and the memory of it is harrowing, recalling as it does the ravages of the brigands' fire.[52]

[52] *Josephus,* trans. H. St. J. Thackeray, Loeb Classical Library (Cambridge, Mass.: Harvard University Press, 1926–65), 3:239–255.

Chapter Two

LAWS AND LEGISLATION

The rabbinic period, from the last centuries before the Common Era to the beginning of the sixth century C.E., was one of the most formative epochs in Jewish history. During these centuries original categories of thought, new evaluations, and fresh modes of action were introduced into Judaism. These innovations, although related to Biblical precedents, differed radically from them. The new institutions, norms of behavior, and rubrics of instruction gradually came to characterize rabbinic Judaism; they constituted the Jewish life style, the pattern of Jewish conduct for generations.

During this period, the basic compilations of rabbinic doctrines and discussions were composed and edited: The Mishnah,[1] Tosefta,[2] both Talmuds [3]—the Jerusalem and Babylonian—and the Midrash.[4] At the same time, the main patterns and forms of synagogal liturgy were developed.

After the fall of Jerusalem, the Rabbis deemed it one of their principal tasks to keep the presence of Jerusalem vividly alive, thereby adding force to the Biblical injunction to set Jerusalem above one's highest joy. They meditated, alone and in groups, on Jerusalem, formulated laws relating to it, interpreted Biblical passages, invented anecdotes and legends,[5] and developed rituals and

[1] Code of Jewish law, compiled and edited by Rabbi Judah the Prince at the end of the second century, C.E.

[2] A parallel collection of Jewish legal matter.

[3] The two principal compendia of rabbinical discussion, containing both legal arguments and rulings (Halakhah) and moral-literary disquisition (Aggadah). See Further Readings.

[4] Collection of rabbinic commentaries on Biblical passages.

[5] See chap. 3.

prayers.[6] They also fostered practices designed to keep Jerusalem alive in the memory of the Jewish people.

No home, they prescribed, was to be without a *zekher leḥurban,* a reminder of the destruction. Accordingly, one wall was to be left unfinished. Many Jews, in addition, decorated the eastern wall of their residence with a *mizraḥ,* a plaque indicating the direction of prayer, for Jews were instructed to face Jerusalem during worship. Such decorations, frequently the only work of art in the house, usually included a sketch of the Western Wall, the Tower of David, and a panoramic, stylized view of Jerusalem.

Times of personal joy were also turned into occasions for the Jews to recall and strengthen this nexus. Soon after the destruction of Jerusalem, certain customs were introduced to commemorate it graphically and clearly. Many bridegrooms on their wedding day placed ashes on their foreheads, and brides refrained from wearing floral headpieces.

> What is meant by "above my chiefest joy" (Psalms 137:6)? R. Isaac said: This is symbolized by the burnt ashes which we place on the head of a bridegroom. R. Papa asked Abaye: "Where should they be placed?" He replied: "Just where the phylactery is worn," as it says: "To give them a garland (*pe'er*) for ashes (*epher*)" (Isaiah 61:3). Whoever mourns for Zion will be privileged to behold her joy, as it says: "Rejoice for joy with her, all you that mourn for her" (Isaiah 66:10).[7]

> During the war of Vespasian they [the Rabbis] forbade the crowns of the bridegroom and the wedding drum. During the war of Titus they forbade the crowns of the brides. . . . In the last war [of Bar Kokhba] they forbade the bride to go forth in a litter inside the city, but our Rabbis permitted the bride to go forth in a litter inside the city.[8]

The blessings recited at the wedding ceremony further underscore this theme.

> Our Rabbis taught: The blessing of the bridegroom is said in the

---

[6] See chap. 4.
[7] *Baba Batra* 60b.
[8] *Mishnah Sotah* 9:14.

presence of ten persons all the seven days following the marriage.[9]

The two blessings which mention Zion are: May Zion rejoice as her children are restored to her in joy. Praised are You, O Lord, who causes Zion to rejoice at her children's return.

O Lord, our God, may there ever be heard in the cities of Judah and in the streets of Jerusalem voices of joy and gladness, voices of bride and bridegroom, the jubilant voices of those joined in marriage under the bridal canopy, the voices of young people feasting and singing.[10]

Regardless of the origin, the breaking of a glass under the wedding canopy came to be understood as a reminder of the destruction of Jerusalem. The *Shulhan Arukh,* compiled by Rabbi Joseph Caro (1488–1575), devotes two paragraphs to this subject, one (*Orah Hayyim,* chap. 560) entitled "To make a reminder of the destruction," and the second (chap. 561), "The rule regarding one who sees the cities of Judah and Jerusalem and the Temple in their ruin." Rabbi Moses Isserles (1520–1572) in his supplements to the Caro text quotes a thirteenth century text (*Kol Bo*): "there are communities in which it is customary to break a glass at the time of the wedding ceremony or to place a black tablecloth. . . ." Rabbi Judah Ashkenazi (first half of eighteenth century) cites a seventeenth-century source relating to the custom of having the groom under the canopy recite verbatim the verse "If I forget thee, Jerusalem."

Distress over Zion's loss was also expressed in wedding music. The following Yemenite song, for example, is sung during the week prior to the wedding.

> O, Lord, proclaim the end of our exile,
> Hasten and gather our remnant . . .
> My beloved, send a redeemer to assemble your people,
> And blast a mighty *shofar* of freedom,
> Quickly build Your ruined Temple,
> Renew our joy and happiness . . .
> We will ascend Mount Zion Your glorious abode
> There to offer our sacrifices.

[9] *Ketubot* 7b–8a.

[10] Jules Harlow, ed. and trans., *A Rabbi's Manual* (New York: The Rabbinical Assembly, © 1965), p. 45. Reprinted by permission of the Rabbinical Assembly.

Other Yemenite wedding customs also recall Jerusalem. In preparation for the marriage ceremony, one of the groom's friends places a platter of dust before the groom. The rabbi takes some on his finger and rubs it on the groom's forehead at the spot where the phylactery is placed and the groom recites: "If I forget thee, Jerusalem . . ."

On the Saturday evening before the wedding, when the groom is adorned in special festal garments, the following is sung:

> Hallelujah, the sound of joy,
>   the sound of merriment,
>   the voice of the groom
>   the voice of the bride
> Rejoice friends and be glad at the wedding,
> For similarly the Lord will announce the
>   five sounds when you ascend to Zion.
> "When you see this your heart shall rejoice,
> Your bones shall flourish like young grass" (Isaiah 66:14).[11]

Jewish burial rites and mourning customs place a similar emphasis on Jerusalem. For millennia pious Jews have instructed their heirs to transfer their remains to *Eretz Yisrael;* in particular they have requested burial in the Mount of Olives in Jerusalem. Others, considered more fortunate, lived their last years in Jerusalem, and were interred there. Every Jew wished to be buried with at least a small bag of soil from *Eretz Yisrael* under his head. These bags were usually filled with earth from the Mount of Olives. Similarly, the potsherds used to cover the eyelids of the deceased were brought by pilgrims from Jerusalem and zealously guarded by their owners.

During bereavement, after the meal of condolence, the grace after meals is recited and in place of the words "Rebuild Jerusalem . . ." etc., the following words of consolation are interpolated.

> O Lord our God, console the mourners of Jerusalem and the mourners of this bereavement. Give them comfort and calm them in their affliction, as it is written: "As a man is comforted by his mother, thus will I comfort you, and in Jerusalem will you be

[11] Joseph Kapah, *Halikhot Teman* (Jerusalem: Hebrew University, 1961), pp. 139–42. My translation.

comforted" (Isaiah 66:13). Praised are you, O Lord, who comforts Zion by rebuilding Jerusalem.

The traditional declaration of solace is: "May the Lord comfort you among the mourners of Zion and Jerusalem."

Sometime during the Gaonic period (after the rabbinic era), the following special paragraph was introduced into the Kaddish to be recited at the graveside after interment.

> Extolled and hallowed be the name of God in that world which He is to create anew, where He will revive the dead, and raise them for everlasting life, rebuild the city of Jerusalem and erect the Temple therein, abolish the worship of idols, and restore the worship of God to its place. Then will the Holy One, praised be He, possess kingship and glory. May this occur during your lifetime and that of the whole house of Israel, speedily and quickly and say Amen.

The Rabbis also regulated the correct conduct for a Jew on entering Jerusalem itself (*Moed Katan* 26a). He who sees the city of Jerusalem in its ruin must say, "Zion is become a wilderness, Jerusalem a desolation" (Isaiah 64:9), and rend his garment. Upon seeing the ruins of the Temple he should say: "Our holy and beautiful house where our fathers praised You is burned with fire; and all our pleasant things are laid waste" (Isaiah 64:10).

The recent reunification of the city brought it under Jewish jurisdiction for the first time in almost two thousand years, and rabbinic authorities ordained that no longer need a Jew rend his garment when he visits Jerusalem or the Western Wall. Instead, he is to offer prayers of thanksgiving, such as the rabbinic formula recited when one comes upon a flourishing Jewish community, namely, "Praised be He who established the border of the widow [Zion]." But since the Temple is not yet restored, rabbinic authorities decree that on seeing the Temple site, one must rend one's garments and pray for its restitution.

There were many other Halakhic rulings dealing with Jerusalem. Some of the most significant follow:

> There are ten degrees of holiness: the Land of Israel is holier than other lands . . . the walled cities of the Land of Israel are

still more holy . . . within the wall of Jerusalem is still more holy, for there only they may eat the Lesser Holy things and the Tithe. The Temple Mount is still more holy. . . . The rampart is still more holy. . . . The Sanctuary is still more holy. . . . The Holy of Holies is still more holy, for none may enter therein save only the High Priest on the Day of Atonement.[12]

> Ten things were said of Jerusalem:
> Jerusalem's houses do not become unclean through leprosy;
> It is not to be declared a condemned city;
> Neither beams nor balconies nor sockets may project there
> over the public thoroughfare lest, by overshadowing, they
> give passage to corpse uncleanness;
> The dead may not be lodged there overnight;
> The bones of a dead man may not be carried through it;
> No place is made available there for a resident alien;
> No graves may be kept there excepting the graves of
> the house of David, and of Ḥuldah the prophetess
> which were there since the days of the early prophets. . . .
> No plants may be planted there, neither gardens nor
> orchards may be cultivated there, excepting rose
> gardens which were there since the days of the
> early prophets;
> Neither geese nor chickens may be raised there, nor,
> needless to say, pigs;
> No dunghills may be kept there because of uncleanness;
> No trial of a stubborn and rebellious son may be held
> there, such is the view of Rabbi Nathan (see Deuteronomy
> 21:18 ff.);
> No houses may be sold there save from the ground up
> [only the structure, not the ground, could be sold];
> The sale of houses is not valid there for longer than
> twelve months;
> No payment for a bed is accepted there [from the
> pilgrims who come for the Festivals]—Rabbi Judah
> says: Not even payment for beds and coverings;
> The hides of the sacrificial beasts are not for sale
> there.[13]

[12] *Mishnah Kelim* 1:6–9.
[13] *The Fathers According to Rabbi Nathan,* trans. Judah Goldin, Yale Judaica Series (New Haven, Conn.: Yale University Press, 1955), chap. 35, pp. 143–144.

If one is standing outside Palestine, he should turn toward *Eretz Yisrael,* . . . if he stands in *Eretz Yisrael* he should turn toward Jerusalem.[14]

One should avoid showing disrespect to the eastern gate [of the Temple] because it is in a direct line with the Holy of Holies. A man should not enter the Temple Mount with his staff or with his shoes on or with his wallet or with his feet dust-stained, nor should he make it a short-cut; spitting there is forbidden *a fortiori.*[15]

All [one's household] may be compelled to go up to Jerusalem [from any other Palestinian place] but none may be compelled to leave [Jerusalem for another city].[16]

They [the Rabbis] then made an ordinance that teachers of children should be appointed in Jerusalem. By what verse did they guide themselves? By the verse: "For from Zion shall the Torah go forth" (Isaiah 2:3). Even so, however, if a child had a father, the father would take him to Jerusalem and have him taught there, and if not, he would not go up to learn there. They therefore ordained that teachers should be appointed in each prefecture.[17]

A woman may not go out on the Sabbath with a golden city. . . . what is meant by "with a golden city"? Rabbah b. Bar Ḥanah said in R. Joḥanan's name: A golden Jerusalem as R. Akiba made for his wife [an ornament with the picture or engraving of Jerusalem on it].[18]

Our Rabbis taught: When the Temple was destroyed for the second time, large numbers in Israel became ascetics, binding themselves neither to eat meat nor to drink wine. R. Joshua got into conversation with them and said to them: "My sons, why do you not eat meat nor drink wine?" They replied: "Shall we eat the flesh which used to be brought as an offering on the altar, now that the altar is not in use? Shall we drink wine which used to be poured as a libation on the altar, but now no longer?" He said to them: "If that is so, we should not eat bread either, because the

---

14 *Berakhot* 30a.
15 *Mishnah Berakhot* 9:5.
16 *Mishnah Ketubot* 13:11.
17 *Baba Batra* 21a.
18 *Shabbat* 59a–b.

meal offerings have ceased." They said: "That is so and we can manage with fruit." "We should not eat fruit either," he said, "because there is no longer an offering of first fruits." "Then we can manage with other fruits," they said. But he said, "We should not drink water because there is no longer any ceremony of the pouring of water." To this they could find no answer, so he said to them: "My sons, come and listen to me. Not to mourn at all is impossible because the blow has fallen. To mourn overmuch is also impossible, because we do not impose on the community a hardship which the community cannot endure, as it is written, 'You are cursed with the curse, yet you rob me, even this whole nation'" (Malachi 3:9). The Sages therefore have ordained thus: A man may stucco his house, but he should leave a little bare. (How much should this be? R. Joseph says: a cubit square, to which R. Hisda adds, that it must be by the door.) A man can prepare a full-course banquet, but he should leave out an item or two. (What should this be? R. Papa says the hors d'oeuvres of salted fish.) A woman can put on all her jewelry but leave off one or two. (What should this be? Rab said not to remove the hair on the temple [which was a mark of elegance].) For so it says: "If I forget you, Jerusalem, let my right hand forget its cunning. Let my tongue cleave to the roof of my mouth, if I remember you not. If I set not Jerusalem above my chiefest joy" (Psalms 137:5–6).[19]

The principal time set aside for mourning both destructions of the Temple was Tishah Be'av, or the Ninth of Av. The period between the Seventeenth of Tammuz and the Ninth of Av is traditionally called "Between the Straits." [20] The following passage gives details on how it is to be observed.

Five things befell our fathers on the Seventeenth of Tammuz and five on the Ninth of Av: On the Seventeenth of Tammuz the Tables of the Ten Commandments were broken. The daily whole offering ceased, the city was breached and Apostomus [unknown figure] burnt the Torah, and an idol was set up in the Sanctuary. On the Ninth of Av it was decreed against our fathers that they should not enter the Land of Israel, the Temple was destroyed the first and second time, Beth-Tor [the site of Bar Kokhba's final de-

19 *Baba Batra* 60b.
20 See below, p. 107.

feat in 135] was captured, and the city was ploughed up. When Av comes in, gladness must be diminished.

In the week wherein falls the Ninth of Av it is forbidden to cut one's hair or wash clothes; but it is permitted on the Thursday because of the honor due the Sabbath. On the eve of the Ninth of Av let none eat of two cooked dishes, let none eat meat and let none drink wine. Rabban Simeon b. Gamaliel says: A man must turn up his couch [i.e., must sleep on the ground]. But the sages did not agree with him.[21]

R. Judah said in the name of Rab: The following was the practice of R. Judah b. Ilai. On the eve of the Ninth of Av dry bread with salt was brought to him and he would take his seat between the baking oven and the cooking stove [i.e., he took up a humble position] and eat. He would drink with it a pitcher full of water and he would appear as if a near relative were lying dead before him.

Elsewhere we have learnt: Where it is the custom to work on the Ninth of Av we may do work, but where it is not the custom we may not, and everywhere the scholars refrain from work. R. Simeon ben Gamaliel says: In this respect a man should always consider himself a scholar. . . . A Baraitha taught: R. Simeon ben Gamaliel says: Anyone who eats or drinks on the Ninth of Av is as if he ate and drank on the Day of Atonement. R. Akiba says: Anyone who does work on the Ninth of Av will never see any sign of blessing in his work. And the sages say: Anyone who does work on the Ninth of Av and does not mourn for Jerusalem will not share in her joy. . . . From this originates what the Rabbis have said: Everyone who mourns for Jerusalem merits to share in her joy, and anyone who does not mourn for her will not share in her joy.[22]

Simon b. Zemaḥ Duran, a practicing physician and noted rabbinical authority, was born in 1361 and died in 1444. The following passage is drawn from one of his many responsa. It deals with Jerusalem's eternal sanctity.

One must study very carefully the degree of sanctity which Jerusalem still retains, as it concerns certain religious obligations which

[21] *Mishnah Ta'anit* 4:6–7.
[22] *Ibid.* 30a–b.

are still applicable and might require Jews to leave other parts of *Eretz Yisrael* and go to Jerusalem. Such an analysis is particularly necessary because it would seem reasonable to assume that since *Eretz Yisrael* has lost its sanctity, Jerusalem's holiness should have also lapsed.

I maintain that even the contention that the holiness of the land at the time of Ezra has lapsed refers only to the rest of *Eretz Yisrael,* but not to Jerusalem and the Temple site. For is it not recorded in Tractate *Zevaḥim* (107b) that three prophets returned from Babylonia and one of them taught that sacrifices are offered even though the Temple has been destroyed . . . ? [Other sources also point to the conclusion] that we must distinguish between the sanctity of *Eretz Yisrael* in general and the sanctity of Jerusalem. The same applies to the rules regarding the walls of Jerusalem. . . . the country's sanctity may lapse, but the sanctity of Jerusalem's walls and the Temple site never lapse, and whosoever enters there even now is punishable by excommunication for there is no means of expiation.

There is a major difference between the sanctity of the land and that of the Temple site, the altar and Jerusalem. The latter are considered holy because of the Divine Presence, for the *Shekhinah* never departed, as we have learned: "I will bring your sanctuaries to desolation" (Leviticus 26:31), and this is further expounded (*Megillah* 28a): "Though they be desolate, they remain sanctified. . . ." This is further attested in the Midrash *Yelamedenu,* "Whether Jerusalem be in ruin or not, the *Shekhinah* yet remains, for it is written, 'Mine eyes and My heart shall be there perpetually' (I Kings 9:3)."

The same view is held by Maimonides, namely that the sanctity of the Temple site is not contingent upon the holiness of the whole land, as he states explicitly in *Hilkhot Bet Ha-Beḥirah* (chap. 6:16).

For practical purposes the Biblical sanctity of *Eretz Yisrael* has lapsed, so that rabbinic ruling only requires us to continue to give gifts and tithes. But the sanctity of Jerusalem has never lapsed.

We may further observe that Jerusalem's sanctity has never terminated, for pilgrims flock to it from Egypt and other countries

. . . and the very same miracles that occurred in Jerusalem during Temple times recur at the present. No one ever claims that the place is too confining. The synagogue which has just enough room for its regular worshipers is filled to overflowing with more than three hundred pilgrims on Shavuot, all of whom find ample room and are seated comfortably. This is so because Jerusalem has retained its sanctity—which is a clear sign of the third redemption.[23]

[23] I. Schzepansky, *Eretz Israel in the Responsa Literature* (Jerusalem: Mosad Harav Kook, 1966), 1:167–70. My translation.

Chapter Three

LEGEND

Halakhah made Jerusalem part of the daily life of the Jew, but it was Aggadah that fired his imagination. Through rabbinic tales, interpretations, and lore touching on every phase of the city's origins and history, Jerusalem remained a living presence for Jews in all the lands of their dispersion.

> He who has not seen Jerusalem in her
> splendor has not seen a desirable
> city in his life.[1]

> There is no wisdom like the wisdom of the
> Land of Israel. There is no beauty like
> the beauty of Jerusalem.[2]

> Jerusalem is the light of the world . . . and
> who is the light of Jerusalem? God.[3]

> There are six things that were chosen: the priestly
> family, the levitical family, Israel, the royal house
> of David, Jerusalem, the Sanctuary.[4]

> Jerusalem is destined to expand until it reaches the
> Throne of Glory.[5]

[1] *Sukkah* 51b. Selections from the Midrash are from *Midrash Rabbah*. See Further Readings.
[2] *The Fathers According to Rabbi Nathan,* chap. 28.
[3] *Genesis Rabbah* 59:5.
[4] *Numbers Rabbah* 3:2.
[5] *Song of Songs Rabbah* 7:5:3.

Ten portions of beauty descended to the world, Jerusalem
acquired nine and the rest of the world one.[6]

Since the day that the Temple was destroyed there has
been no day without its curse; the dew has not fallen
in blessing and fruits have lost their savor.[7]

When Jerusalem is built David will come . . . and when
David comes, prayer will come . . . and when prayer comes,
the Temple service will return.[8]

Jerusalem will be redeemed only by
righteousness.[9]

When anyone prays in Jerusalem it is as
if he worshiped before the Throne of Glory,
for the gate to heaven is there and it is
wide open for the Lord to hear.[10]

Since the day Jerusalem was destroyed there
has been no joy before the Lord, [there will be none] until He
rebuilds it and restores the Jewish people to it.[11]

The construction of the earth was begun at the center with the
foundation stone of the Temple, the *Even Shetiyah*. For the Holy
Land is at the central point of the surface of the earth, Jerusalem
is at the central point of Palestine, and the Temple is situated at
the center of the Holy City.[12]

The body of man is a microcosm, the whole world in miniature,
and the world in turn is a reflex of man. The hair upon his head
corresponds to the woods of the earth, his tears to a river, his
mouth to the ocean. The world resembles the ball of his eye; the
ocean that encircles the earth is like the white of the eye, the dry

[6] *Kiddushin* 49b.
[7] *Mishnah Sotah* 9:12.
[8] *Megillah* 17b–18a.
[9] *Sabbat* 139a.
[10] *Pirke de Rabbi Eliezer* 35.
[11] *Yalqut, Ekah,* 1009.
[12] Louis Ginzberg, *The Legends of the Jews,* 1:12. See Further Readings.

land is the iris, Jerusalem the pupil, and the Temple the image mirrored in the pupil of the eye.[13]

When day began to dawn [Adam] brought an offering unto God, a unicorn whose horn was created before his hoofs, and he sacrificed it on the spot on which later the altar was to stand in Jerusalem.[14]

The place on which Abraham had erected the altar was the same whereon Adam had brought the first sacrifice and [whereon] Cain and Abel had offered their gift to God—the same whereon Noah raised an altar to God after he left the ark; and Abraham, who knew that it was the place appointed for the Temple, called it *Yireh* for it would be the abiding place of the fear and service of God. But as Shem had given it the name *Shalem*, place of peace, and God would not give offense to either Abraham or Shem, He united the two names, and called the city by the name Jerusalem.[15]

David's first thought after ascending the throne was to wrest Jerusalem, sacred since the days of Adam, Noah and Abraham, from the grasp of the heathen. The plan was not easy of execution for various reasons. The Jebusites, the possessors of Jerusalem, were the posterity of those sons of Heth who ceded the cave of Machpelah to Abraham only on condition that their descendants should never be forcibly dispossessed of their capital city Jerusalem. In perpetuation of this agreement between Abraham and the sons of Heth, monuments of brass were erected, and when David approached Jerusalem with hostile intent, the Jebusites pointed to Abraham's promise engraven upon them and still plainly to be read. They maintained that before David could take the city, which they had surrounded with a high wall, he would have to destroy the monuments. Joab devised a plan of getting into Jerusalem. He set up a tall cypress tree near the wall, bent it downward, and

[13] *Ibid.*, pp. 49–50.

[14] *Ibid.*, p. 89. Professor Ginzberg comments: "That Adam erected an altar on Mount Moriah cannot be considered strange; since not only was the dust, used for the formation of his body, taken from the same place, but it was also this mountain on which he landed after the expulsion from paradise, because the gate of Moriah is found in the proximity of paradise, and Adam was buried in the same place, in the site of the altar at Jerusalem" (5:117, n. 109).

[15] *Ibid.*, p. 285.

standing on David's head, he grasped the very tip of the tree. When
the tree rebounded, Joab sat high above the wall, and could jump
down on it. Once in the city, he destroyed the monuments and
possessed himself of Jerusalem. For David, a miracle had happened; the wall lowered itself before him so that he could walk
into the city without difficulty. David, however, was not desirous
of using forcible means. He, therefore, offered the Jebusites six
hundred shekels, fifty shekels for each Israelite tribe. The Jebusites
accepted the money and gave David a bill of sale.[16]

As the Rabbis read and reread the Bible, Jerusalem rarely left
their thoughts.

Rabbi Ḥanina b. Papa said, the Holy One, praised be He, wished
to give Jerusalem a definite size for it is said "To measure Jerusalem" (Zechariah 2:6). The ministering angels said before the Holy
One, praised be He, "Lord of the Universe, You have created
many towns for the nations of the earth and You did not fix
their length or breadth; will You limit the measurements of Jerusalem in the midst of which is Your name, Your sanctuary and
the righteous?" Thereupon an angel responded: "Jerusalem shall
be inhabited without walls" (Zechariah 2:8).[17]

Rabbi Nehemiah interpreted: [Genesis 49:11] "Binding *iro* [his
foal] unto the vine" means: He [God] binds *iro*—his city—Jerusalem—to the vine—Israel.[18]

Rabbi Simeon b. Yoḥai made the following comment on "He
stands and measures the earth . . ." (Habakkuk 3:6). The Holy
One, praised be He, measured the generations and found no people fitted to receive the Torah other than the generation of the
wilderness. . . . He considered all cities and found no city
wherein the Temple might be built, other than Jerusalem.[19]

"There are threescore queens and fourscore concubines" (Song of
Songs 6:8) is interpreted by the Rabbis to mean, the sixty tractates
of the Talmud and the eighty houses of study that flourished in
Jerusalem. This number corresponds to Jerusalem's gates.[20]

16 *Ibid.*, 4:91–92.
17 *Baba Batra* 75b.
18 *Genesis Rabbah* 98:9.
19 *Leviticus Rabbah* 13:2.
20 *Numbers Rabbah* 18:21.

On Psalms 128:5, "The Lord bless you out of Zion," the Rabbis said: This teaches that the Holy One, praised be He, will bless you from the same place as that from which He blessed Israel. How do you know that blessings emanate from Zion? Because it says: "For there [Zion] the Lord commanded the blessing" (Psalms 133:3), and it says: "The Lord bless you out of Zion . . ." (Psalms 128:5) is an assurance that they will be privileged to see the good of Jerusalem in the Messianic era.[21]

"The hallowed stones are poured out" (Lamentations 4:1), . . . an allusion to the men of Jerusalem who were like a golden ornament—and their bodies like precious stones and pearls . . .
   "The precious sons of Zion" (Lamentations 4:2). In what did their precious character consist? When a man of one of the other Palestinian towns married a woman of Jerusalem he gave her her weight in gold; and when a Jerusalemite married a woman from another town he received his weight in gold. Another explanation of their precious character: When a man of Jerusalem married a woman of superior status to his own, he made the tables arranged for the wedding feast more costly than the expenditure on his domestic furnishings, and when she was of inferior status, he made his expenditure on his domestic furnishings more costly than the tables arranged for the wedding feast. Another explanation of their precious character: none of them would attend a banquet until he was invited twice.[22]

There were special commentaries relating to Jerusalem during Festivals, when the population was swollen by pilgrims.

"The city that was full of people" (Lamentations 1:1). Rabbi Samuel taught: There were twenty-four thoroughfares in Jerusalem. Each thoroughfare had twenty-four sideturnings; each sideturning had twenty-four roads, each road had twenty-four streets, each street had twenty-four courts, each court had twenty-four houses; and each court residents double the number of those who came out of Egypt.[23]

Rabbi Abin son of Rabbi Adda said in Rabbi Isaac's name: Why are there no fruits of Genassaret [Kinneret] in Jerusalem? So that

[21] *Ibid.* 8:9.
[22] *Lamentations Rabbah* 4:1–2.
[23] *Ibid.* 1:2.

the Festival pilgrims should not say, "Had we merely ascended in order to eat the fruits of Genassaret in Jerusalem it would have sufficed us," with the result that the pilgrimage would not be for its own sake. Similarly Rabbi Dosethai son of Rabbi Jannai said: Why are the thermal springs of Tiberias not found in Jerusalem? So that Festival pilgrims should not say, "Had we merely ascended in order to bathe in the thermal springs of Tiberias, it would have sufficed us," with the result that the pilgrimage would not be for its own sake.[24]

Ten wonders were wrought for our fathers in the Temple: no woman miscarried through the smell of the flesh of sacrifices, no sacrificial meat ever turned putrid, no fly was seen in the shambles, the High Priest never suffered a pollution on the Day of Atonement, rains never quenched the fires of the woodpile on the altar, no wind prevailed over the pillar of smoke, never was a defect found in the Omer, or in the two loaves, or in the showbread; the people stood pressed together yet bowed themselves at ease, neither serpent nor scorpion ever harmed anyone in Jerusalem, and no man said to his fellow, "The place is too confined for me that I should [not] lodge in Jerusalem." [25]

The Rabbis frequently wrestled with the problem of explaining why the First Temple had been destroyed, and their imaginations conjured up all kinds of phenomena to accompany the disaster.

Why was the first Sanctuary destroyed? Because of the three evils which prevailed there, idolatry, immorality, and bloodshed. . . . Therefore, the Holy One, praised be He, brought them three evil decrees as against the three evils which were their own.[26]

Raba son of Rabbi Ilai lectured: What is meant by "Moreover the Lord said, because the daughters of Zion are haughty" (Isaiah 3:16)? That means that they walked with haughty bearing. "Walk with outstretched necks"—they walked heel by toe. "And wanton eyes"—they filled their eyes with stibium and beckoned to the men. . . . "And making a tinkling with their feet," Rabbi Isaac of the school of R. Ammi said: This teaches that they placed myrrh and balsam on their shoes and walked through the market-places of

---

[24] *Pesaḥim* 8b.
[25] *Abot* 5:5.
[26] *Yoma* 9b.

Jerusalem and on coming near the young men of Israel, they
kicked their feet and spurted it on them; thus instilling them with
passionate desire like with serpent's poison. What is their punishment? . . . The place where they perfumed themselves shall be
decaying sores.

Rahabah said in R. Judah's name: The fuel logs of Jerusalem
were of the cinnamon tree and when lit their fragrance pervaded
the whole of *Eretz Yisrael,* but when Jerusalem was destroyed
they were hidden, only as much as a barley grain being left, which
is to be found in the queen's collection of rarities.[27]

Our Rabbis taught: When the First Temple was about to be
destroyed, bands upon bands of young priests with the keys of the
Temple in their hands assembled and mounted the roof of the
Temple and exclaimed, "Master of the Universe, as we did not
have the merit to be faithful custodians, these keys are handed
back into Your keeping." They then threw the keys up toward
heaven. And there emerged the figure of a hand and received the
keys from them. Whereupon they jumped and fell into the fire.[28]

For eighteen years daily a heavenly voice resounded in the palace of Nebuchadnezzar, saying: "O you wicked slave, go and destroy the house of your Lord, for His children hearken not to
Him." But Nebuchadnezzar was beset with fears lest God prepare
a fate for him similar to that of his ancestor Sennacherib. He prac-
ticed belomancy and consulted other auguries, to assure himself
that the war against Jerusalem would result favorably. When he
shook up the arrows, and questioned whether he was to go to
Rome or Alexandria, not one arrow sprang up, but when he questioned about Jerusalem, one sprang up. He sowed seeds and set
out plants; for Rome or Alexandria nothing came up; for Jerusalem everything sprouted and grew. He lighted candles and lanterns;
for Rome or Alexandria they refused to burn, for Jerusalem they
shed their light. He floated vessels on the Euphrates; for Rome
or Alexandria they did not move, for Jerusalem they swam.

Still the fears of Nebuchadnezzar were not allayed. His deter-
mination to attack the Holy City ripened only after God Himself
had shown him how He had bound the hands of the archangel
Michael, the patron of the Jews, behind his back, in order to

[27] *Shabbat* 62b–63a.
[28] *Ta'anit* 29a.

render him powerless to bring aid to his wards. So the campaign against Jerusalem was undertaken.[29]

You find that when Nebuzaradan came up to destroy Jerusalem, the Holy One, blessed be He, hinted to that blood [of Zechariah] that it should seethe and bubble for two hundred and fifty-two years from the reign of Joash to that of Zedekiah. What did they do? They scraped quantities of dust to throw on it and made heaps and heaps over it, but it did not become still, and the blood kept seething and foaming. The Holy One, blessed be He, said to the blood: "The time has come for you to collect your debt." When Nebuzaradan came up and saw it, he asked, "What kind of blood is this which seethes in this manner?" They answered, "The blood of bulls, rams, and lambs which are slaughtered and offered as sacrifices." He had bulls, rams, and lambs brought and slaughtered alongside of it, but it did not become still or rest or stop seething. He forthwith took and hanged them on the gallows, saying to them, "Tell me what is the nature of this blood, otherwise I will comb your flesh with an iron comb." They replied, "Since the Holy One, blessed be He, is determined to demand punishment from us for his blood, we will reveal to you what happened. There was a priest-prophet and judge who prophesied against us all that you are doing with us; but we did not believe him, and we arose against him and killed him because he reproved us." Nebuzaradan immediately had eighty thousand priestly novitiates brought and slew them by it. The blood did not stop, but gushed forth until it reached the grave of Zechariah. He took the Great Sanhedrin and Minor Sanhedrin and slew them by it; but it did not stop. Then the villain went and exclaimed over the blood, "Are you and your blood better than these men and their blood? Do you wish me to destroy all your people on their account!" At that moment the Holy One, blessed be He, was filled with compassion and said, "If this wicked and cruel person, son of a wicked father, who came up to destroy My house, is filled with compassion for them, how much more should I be so of whom it is written, The Lord, the Lord, God, merciful and gracious (Exodus 34:6), and, The Lord is good to all, and His tender mercies are over all His works (Psalms 145:9)!" . . . R. Judan said; Seven transgressions were committed by Israel at that time: they killed a

29 Ginzberg, *Legends,* 4:300–1.

priest, a prophet, and a judge, they shed innocent blood, they defiled
the Temple Court, and this was done on the Sabbath which was also
the Day of Atonement.[30]

The most extensive rabbinic commentary is, understandably,
based on Lamentations.

The Holy One, blessed be He, said to the ministering angels,
"Come, let us go together and see what the enemy has done to
My house." Forthwith the Holy One, blessed be He, and the ministering angels went, Jeremiah leading the way. When the Holy
One, blessed be He, saw the Temple, He said, "Certainly this is
My house and this is My resting place into which enemies have
come, and they have done with it whatever they wished." At that
time the Holy One, blessed be He, wept and said, "Woe is Me
for My house! My children, where are you? My priests, where
are you? My lovers, where are you? What shall I do with you,
seeing that I warned you but you did not repent?" The Holy One,
blessed be He, said to Jeremiah, "I am now like a man who had
an only son, for whom he prepared a marriage-canopy, but he
died under it. Do you feel no anguish for Me and My children?
Go, summon Abraham, Isaac and Jacob, and Moses from their
sepulchres, for they know how to weep." . . .
There and then Jeremiah went to the cave of Machpelah and
said to the patriarchs of the world: "Arise, for the time has come
when your presence is required before the Holy One, blessed be
He." They said to him, "For what purpose?" He answered, "I know
not," because he was afraid lest they say, "In your lifetime has
such a thing happened to our children!" Jeremiah left them, and
stood by the bank of the Jordan and called out, "Son of Amram,
son of Amram, arise, the time has come when your presence is
required before the Holy One, blessed be He." He said to him,
"How is this day different from other days that my presence is
required before the Holy One, blessed be He?" Jeremiah replied,
"I know not." Moses left him and proceeded to the ministering
angels whom he recognized from the time of the giving of the
Torah. He said to them, "O celestial ministers, know you why
my presence is required before the Holy One, blessed be He?"
They replied, "Son of Amram, do you not know that the Temple

[30] *Ecclesiastes Rabbah* 3:16.

is destroyed and Israel gone into exile?" He cried aloud and wept until he reached the patriarchs. They immediately also rent their garments, placed their hands upon their heads, and cried out and wept until they arrived at the gates of the Temple. When the Holy One, blessed be He, saw them, immediately he said: "In that day did the Lord, the God of hosts, call to weeping, and to lamentation, and to baldness, and to girding with sackcloth" (Isaiah 22:12). Were it not explicitly stated in Scripture, it would be impossible to say such a thing, but they went weeping from one gate to another like a man whose dead is lying before him, and the Holy One, blessed be He, lamented saying, "Woe to the King who succeeded in His youth but failed in His old age!" . . .

The Holy One, blessed be He, said to Abraham, "Let the twenty-two letters come and testify against Israel." Forthwith the twenty-two letters appeared. The *aleph* came to testify that Israel had transgressed the Torah. Abraham said to it, "You, *aleph,* are the first of all the letters, and you come to testify against Israel in the day of their trouble! Remember the day when the Holy One, blessed be He, revealed Himself upon Mount Sinai and opened with you, I am the Lord your God (Exodus 20:2), and no nation accepted you but my children, and you come to testify against my children!" The *aleph* immediately stood aside and gave no testimony against them. The *bet* came to testify against Israel, and Abraham said to it, "My daughter, you come to testify against my children who were zealous about the Pentateuch of which you are the first letter, as it is written, In the beginning God created . . . (Genesis 1:1)." The *bet* immediately stood aside and gave no testimony against them. The *gimel* came to testify against Israel, and Abraham said to it, *"Gimel,* you are come to testify against my children that they transgressed the Torah! Is there a nation which observes the commandment of fringes, of which you are the first letter, except my children; as it is written, you shall make yourself twisted cords (Deuteronomy 22:12)!" The *gimel* immediately stood aside and gave no testimony against them.

When the remainder of the letters saw that Abraham silenced these, they felt ashamed and stood apart and did not testify against Israel. Abraham thereupon began to speak before the Holy One, blessed be He, saying, "Sovereign of the Universe, when I was a hundred years old You gave me a son, and when he reached years of discretion and was a young man of thirty-seven, You ordered me, 'Offer him as a sacrifice before Me.' I steeled my heart against him and I had no compassion on him; but I myself bound him. Will You not remember this on my behalf and have mercy on my children?" Isaac began, saying, "Sovereign of the Universe, when my father said to me, 'God will provide Himself the lamb for a burnt-offering, my son' (Genesis 22:8), I raised no objection to the carrying out of Your words, and I willingly let myself be bound on the top of the altar and stretched out my neck beneath the knife. Will You not remember this on my behalf and have mercy on my children?" Jacob began, saying, "Sovereign of the Universe, did I not stay twenty years in Laban's house? And when I left his house, the wicked Esau met me and sought to kill my children, and I risked my life on their behalf. Now they are delivered into the hands of their enemies like sheep to the slaughter, after I reared them like chickens and endured for their sakes the pain of child-rearing. For throughout most of my days I experienced great trouble on their account. Now, will You not remember this on my behalf to have mercy on my children?" Moses began, saying, "Sovereign of the Universe, was I not a faithful shepherd to Israel for forty years, running before them like a horse in the desert? When the time arrived for them to enter the promised land, You decreed against me that my bones should fall in the wilderness. Now that they are exiled, You have sent for me to lament and weep over them. This bears out the popular proverb, 'I derive no benefit from my master's good fortune, but suffer from his bad fortune.' " . . .

Moses further spoke before Him: "Sovereign of the Universe, You have written in Your Torah, Whether it be a cow or ewe, you shall not kill it and its young both in one day (Leviticus 22:28); but have they killed many, many mothers and sons, and You are silent!" At that moment, the matriarch Rachel broke forth into speech before the Holy One, blessed be He, and said, "Sovereign of the Universe, it is revealed before You that Your servant Jacob loved me exceedingly and toiled for my father on my behalf seven years. When those seven years were completed and the time arrived for my marriage with my husband, my father planned to substitute another for me to wed my husband for the sake of my sister. It was very hard for me, because the plot was known to me and I disclosed it to my husband; and I gave him a sign whereby he could distinguish between me and my sister, so that my father should not be able to make the substitution. After that I relented, suppressed my desire, and had pity upon my sister that she should not be exposed to shame. In the evening they substituted my sister for me with my husband, and I delivered over to my sister all the signs which I had arranged with my husband so that he should think that she was Rachel. More than that, I went beneath the bed upon which he lay with my sister; and when he spoke to her she remained silent and I made all the replies in order that he should not recognize my sister's voice. I did her a kindness, was not jealous of her, and did not expose her to shame. And if I, a creature of flesh and blood, formed of dust and ashes, was not envious of my rival and did not expose her to shame and contempt, why should You, a King who lives eternally and is merciful, be jealous of idolatry in which there is no reality, and exile my children and let them be slain by the sword, and their enemies have done with them as they wished!"

Forthwith the mercy of the Holy One, blessed be He, was stirred, and He said, "For Your sake, Rachel, I will restore Israel to their place." And so it is written, Thus says the Lord: A voice is heard in Ramah, lamentation and bitter weeping, Rachel weeping for her children; she refuses to be comforted for her children (Jeremiah 31:15). This is followed by, Thus says the Lord: Refrain your voice from weeping, and your eyes from tears; for your work shall be rewarded . . . and there is hope for your future, says the Lord; and your children shall return to their own border (*Ibid.* 16–17).[31]

"I watch and am become like a sparrow." (Psalms 102:8) The Holy One, praised be He, said "I watched carefully to cause My *Shekhinah* to abide in the Temple forever. And I am become like a sparrow: just as when you take away its young a sparrow is left solitary," so spoke the Holy One, praised be He. "I burnt My house, destroyed My city, exiled My children among the nations of the world and I sit solitary." [32]

A separate set of explanations were worked out for the destruction of the Second Temple.

The destruction of Jerusalem came through a Kamza and a Bar Kamza in this way. A certain man had a friend Kamza and an

31 *Lamentations Rabbah,* Proems, chap. 24.
32 *Ibid.,* chap. 20.

enemy Bar Kamza. He once made a party and said to his servant, Go and bring Kamza. The man went and brought Bar Kamza. When the man [who gave the party] found him there he said, "See, you tell tales about me; what are you doing here? Get out." Said the other: "Since I am here, let me stay, and I will pay you for whatever I eat and drink." He said, "I won't." "Then let me give you half the cost of the party." "No," said the other. "Then let me pay for the whole party." He still said, "No," and he took him by the hand and put him out. Said the other, "Since the Rabbis were sitting there and did not stop him this shows that they agreed with him. I will go and inform against them to the Government." He went and said to the emperor, "The Jews are rebelling against you." He said, "How can I know this?" He said to him: "Send them an offering and see whether they will offer it [on the altar]." So [the emperor] sent with [Bar Kamza] a fine calf. While on the way he made a blemish on its upper lip, or as some say on the white of its eye, in a place where we [Jews] count it a blemish but they do not. The Rabbis were inclined to offer it in order not to offend the Government. Said R. Zechariah b. Abkulas to them: "People will say that blemished animals are offered on the altar." They then proposed to kill Bar Kamza so that he should not go and inform against them, but R. Zechariah b. Abkulas said to them, "Is one who makes a blemish on consecrated animals to be put to death?" R. Johanan thereupon remarked: "Through the scrupulousness of R. Zechariah b. Abkulas our House has been destroyed, our Temple burnt and we ourselves exiled from our land."

It has been taught: Note from this incident how serious a thing it is to put a man to shame, for God espoused the cause of Bar Kamza and destroyed His House and burnt His Temple.[33]

Now when the Emperor Vespasian came to destroy Jerusalem the zealots sought to burn all that wealth of Kalba Sabua's in fire. Kalba Sabua said to them: Why are you destroying this city and why do you seek to burn all that wealth in fire? Give me time to go and see what I have in the house.

He went and found that he had food for twenty-two years enough for a feast for each and every one in Jerusalem. Thereupon he gave orders that food be heaped up and sorted out and sifted and kneaded and baked and prepared for twenty-two years for

[33] *Gittin* 55b–57a.

each and every one in Jerusalem. But they paid no attention to him.

What did the men of Jerusalem do? They would bring loaves and brick them into the walls and plaster them over with clay.

The men of Jerusalem did yet another thing: they would boil straw and eat it.

And everyone in Israel stationed at the walls of Jerusalem would exclaim: "Someone give me five dates and I will go and capture five heads!" When given five dates, he would go down and capture five heads of Vespasian's men.

As Vespasian looked at their excrement and saw that there was in it no sign of corn he said to his troops: "If those who eat nothing but straw kill a number of you in this fashion, how they would kill you if they ate everything you eat and drink!" [34]

On one occasion R. Gamaliel, R. Elezar b. Azariah, R. Joshua, and R. Akiba were coming up to Jerusalem, and when they reached Mount Scopus they rent their garments. When they arrived at the Temple Mount, they saw a fox emerging from the Holy of Holies. They fell a-weeping, but R. Akiba laughed. They said, "Akiba, you always surprise us. We weep and you are merry!" He replied, "Wherefore are you weeping?" They answered, "Shall we not weep that from a place of which it was written, And the common man that draws nigh shall be put to death (Numbers 1:51), a fox emerges, and concerning it the verse is fulfilled. For the Mountain of Zion, which is desolate, the foxes walk upon it (Lamentations 5:18)?" He said: "For that reason am I merry, Behold, it states, And I will take unto Me faithful witnesses to record, Uriah the priest, and Zechariah, the son of Jeberechiah (Isaiah 8:2). Now what connection has Uriah with Zechariah? Uriah lived in the time of the First Temple while Zechariah lived in the time of the Second Temple! But what did Uriah say? Thus says the Lord of hosts: Zion shall be plowed as a field, and Jerusalem shall become heaps (Jeremiah 26:18). And what did Zechariah say? There shall yet old men and old women sit in the broad places of Jerusalem, every man with his staff in his hand for very age (Zechariah 8:4); and it continues, And the broad places of the city shall be full of boys and girls playing in the broad places thereof (*Ibid.* 5). The Holy One, blessed be He, said, 'Behold, I have these two witnesses, and if the words of Uriah are fulfilled,

[34] *Rabbi Nathan,* chap. 6, pp. 45–46.

the words of Zechariah will be fulfilled; and if the words of Uriah prove vain the words of Zechariah will prove vain.' I rejoiced because the words of Uriah have been fulfilled and in the future the words of Zechariah will be fulfilled." Thereupon in these terms did they address him: "Akiba, you have consoled us; may you be comforted by the coming of the herald [of the redemption]!" [35]

Once as Rabbi Joḥanan ben Zakkai was coming forth from Jerusalem, Rabbi Joshua followed after him and beheld the Temple in ruins. "Woe unto us," R. Joshua cried, "that this, the place where the iniquities of Israel were atoned for, is laid waste!"

"My son," R. Joḥanan said to him, "be not grieved, we have another atonement as effective as this. And what is it? It is acts of loving-kindness as it is said, 'For I desire mercy and not sacrifice' (Hosea 6:6)." [36]

It has been taught: R. Jose says, I was once traveling on the road and I entered into one of the ruins of Jerusalem in order to pray. Elijah of blessed memory appeared and waited at the door till I finished my prayer. . . . He said to me: "My son, what sound did you hear in the ruin?" I replied: "I heard a divine voice cooing like a dove and saying: 'Woe to the children on account of whose sins I destroyed My house and burnt My temple and exiled them among the nations of the world!' He said to me, 'By your life and by your head! not in this moment alone does it so exclaim, but thrice each day does it exclaim thus.'" [37]

For Jews, Jerusalem, despite its physical destruction, could never really be destroyed.

> The Holy One, praised be He, is destined to add to Jerusalem as far as a horse can run and cast its shadow.[38]

> What is left of leviathan's skin will be stretched out over Jerusalem as a canopy, and the light streaming from it will illumine the whole world.[39]

[35] *Lamentations Rabbah* 5:18.
[36] *Rabbi Nathan,* chap. 4, p. 34.
[37] *Berakhot* 3a.
[38] *Pesaḥim* 50a.
[39] Ginzberg, *Legends,* 1:28.

"We will be glad and rejoice in you" (Song of Songs 1:4).
They are like a queen whose husband, the king, [and] whose sons
and sons-in-law went abroad. When they come and tell her, "Your
sons have returned," she replies, "What is that to me? Let my
daughters-in-law rejoice." When her sons-in-law return and they
tell her, "Your sons-in-law are here," she replies, "What is that to
me? Let my daughters rejoice." But when they say to her, "The
king, your husband, has returned," she says, "This is a real pleasure, joy on joy." So in time to come the prophets will come and
say to Jerusalem, "Your sons come from far!" (Isaiah 60:4), and
she will reply, "What is that to me?" When they say, "And your
daughters are borne on the side," she will say, "What is that to
me?" But when they will say to her, "Behold, your king comes
unto you, he is triumphant and victorious" (Zechariah 9:9), she
will say, "This is a real joy," as it is written, "Rejoice greatly,
O daughter of Zion" (*Ibid.* 9:9), and it is also written, "Sing and
rejoice, O daughter of Zion" (*Ibid.* 2:14). At that moment she
will say, "I will greatly rejoice in the Lord, my soul shall be joy-
ful in my God" (Isaiah 61:10).[40]

"Daughters of Jerusalem." R. Joḥanan said, Jerusalem will one
day become the metropolis of all countries and draw people to
her in streams to do her honor.[41]

"Builded with turrets" (*Talpiot*) (Song of Songs 4:4). Ḥiyya b.
R. Bun said: It means that what was once beauty [*yafe*] has been
turned into a ruin [*tel*]. Said the Holy One, praised be He: It is
I who made it a ruin in this world; it is I who will make it a
thing of beauty in the world to come.

Another explanation: *Talpiot,* the ruin [*tel*] for which all mouths
[*piyot*] pray. Hence it was laid down: Those who stand up to
pray outside the Land of Israel turn their faces to the Land of
Israel. . . . Those who pray in the Land of Israel turn toward Jerusalem.[42]

"When the Lord shall enlarge your border" (Deuteronomy
12:20). The Rabbis say this refers to Jerusalem. Only when God
will enlarge it will the full prosperity of Jerusalem become
known.[43]

[40] *Song of Songs Rabbah* 1:4:2.
[41] *Ibid.* 1:5:3.
[42] *Ibid.* 4:4:9.
[43] *Deuteronomy Rabbah* 4:11.

Resh Lakish said: The Holy One, praised be He, will in time to come add to Jerusalem a thousand gardens, a thousand towers, a thousand palaces, a thousand mansions, and each of these will be as large as Sepphoris in its prosperity. It has been taught: R. Jose said, I saw Sepphoris in its prosperity and it contained 180,000 markets for pudding dealers.

It is written: "And the side chambers were one over another three and thirty times" (Ezekiel 41:6): What is meant by three and thirty times? R. Levi in the name of R. Papi in the name of R. Joshua of Siknin said: If in time to come there will be three Jerusalems [i.e. Jerusalem will be three times the size of the present Jerusalem] each building will contain thirty dwellings one over the other; and if there will be thirty Jerusalems [i.e. Jerusalem will be thirty times its present size] each building will contain three dwellings one over the other.[44]

"And your gates of carbuncles" (Isaiah 54:12) is to be understood as R. Johanan explained when he once sat and gave exposition: The Holy One, praised be He, will in time to come bring precious stones and pearls which are thirty cubits by thirty cubits and will cut out from them openings to serve as entrances to the city, ten cubits by twenty and will set them up in the gates of Jerusalem. A certain student sneered at him: "Jewels of the size of a dove's egg are not to be found: are jewels of such a size to be found?" After a time his ship sailed out to sea where he saw ministering angels engaged in cutting precious stones and pearls which were thirty cubits by thirty and on which were engravings of ten cubits by twenty. He said to them: "For whom are these?" They replied that the Holy One, praised be He, would in time to come set them up in the gates of Jerusalem.[45]

One of the ideas that arose as a result of the destruction of the Temple and the expulsion of the Jew from Jerusalem was the view that parallel to the earthly Jerusalem there exists a celestial ideal, "Jerusalem on high," said to have been established before the creation of the world. This ethereal Jerusalem is eternally preserved in all its pristine splendor. While for two millennia the Jews were prevented from reconstructing the earthly Jerusalem, they devoted themselves to envisaging the supernatural Jerusalem.

[44] *Baba Batra* 75b.
[45] *Ibid.* 75a.

Needless to say, they never betrayed the terrestrial Jerusalem for the sake of the "ideal" Jerusalem. The following conversation between R. Naḥman, a Babylonian scholar of the fourth century, and his colleague, R. Isaac, a Palestinian preacher, attests to the priority of the earthly Jerusalem over its celestial counterpart. Replying to R. Naḥman's query, R. Isaac quotes R. Joḥanan, a Palestinian scribe of the second half of the third century: "The Holy One, praised be He, declared, 'I shall enter heavenly Jerusalem only after I have entered the Jerusalem on earth.' " [46]

Medieval Biblical exegetes continually read into the Bible contemporary political events while avidly searching recondite passages for clues to "the end of days." The *midreshei geulah*—homilies of redemption—abound with intricate and cryptic attempts to fathom the final catastrophe heralding the eventual, crowning redemption.

Many Jews anticipated that the Arab conquerors of the seventh century would deliver them from Christian servitude. The numerous apocalypses of this period attest to these yearnings. In an apocalyptic Midrash which some scholars date from the eighth century we read a detailed description of the daily events which were allegedly revealed to Elijah on Mount Carmel. These events were to culminate in cosmic wars that would destroy the nations of the world and cast the Jewish people into the depths of degradation. Such cataclysmic catastrophes were the necessary prelude to a Messianic period that was to usher in a new and glorious era for the Jewish people, crowned by the rebuilding of Jerusalem.

> Elijah said: I behold a massive, magnificent, glorious, lofty rebuilt city lowered from the heavens . . . rebuilt and perfected, her people once again residing therein, the city itself perched upon three thousand towers. The space between each tower measuring twenty ris and that space filled by twenty-five thousand spans of emeralds, jewels and pearls as it is predicted, "I will make your pinnacles as rubies, your gates of carbuncles, all your borders of precious stones."
> Elijah continued: I see the homes and passageways of the righteous, their thresholds and doorposts made of precious stones.

[46] *Ta'anit* 5a.

The treasures of the Temple overflow to their doorways. Torah and peace abide among them in fulfillment of the predictions: "All your children shall be taught of the Lord, and great shall be your children's peace" (Isaiah 54:13).[47]

The telling and retelling of legends centering about Jerusalem and its holy character continued all through Jewish history. For example, the folklore of Ḥasidism, a major mystical movement originating in Eastern Europe in the eighteenth century, is rich in anecdotes pertaining to the Golden City, which became a center for Ḥasidic immigration in the nineteenth century.

A typical Ḥasidic saying is that of the Ropshitzer Rebbe: "By our service to God," he used to affirm, "we build Jerusalem daily. One of us adds a row, another only a brick. When Jerusalem is completed, redemption will come."

[47] Y. Ibn-Shmuel, ed., *Midreshei Geulah* (Jerusalem: Mosad Bialik, 1954; Ramat-Gan: Massada, 1954), p. 48. Reprinted by permission of the publishers. (My translation.)

Chapter Four

SONG, POEM, PRAYER

Psalms, a section of Writings in the Bible, were included in the liturgy at an early date.

A Song; a Psalm of the sons of Koraḥ.

Great is the Lord, and highly to be praised,
In the city of our God, His holy mountain.
Beautiful scene, the joy of the whole earth,
Mount Zion, the uttermost parts of the north,
The city of the great King.
God in her palaces
Has made Himself known for a stronghold.

We have thought of Your loving kindness, O God,
In the midst of Your temple,
As is Your name, O God,
So is Your praise unto the ends of the earth;
Your right hand is full of righteousness.
Let Mount Zion be glad,
Let the daughters of Judah rejoice,
Because of Your judgments.
Walk about Zion, and go round about her;
Count the towers thereof.
Mark well her ramparts,
Traverse her palaces;
That You may tell it to the generation following.
For such is God, our God, for ever and ever,
He will guide us eternally.[1]

[1] Ps. 48.

A Psalm of the sons of Koraḥ; a Song.

His foundation is in the holy mountains.
The Lord loves the gates of Zion
More than all the dwellings of Jacob.
Glorious things are spoken of you, O city of God. Selah.
"I will make mention of Rahab and Babylon as among them
    that know Me;
Behold Philistia, and Tyre, and Ethiopia,
This one was born there."
But of Zion it shall be said: "This man and that was
    born in her;
And the Most High Himself establishes her."
The Lord shall count in the register of the peoples:
"This one was born there." Selah.
And whether they sing or dance,
All my thoughts are in you.[2]

A Song of Ascents: of David

I rejoiced when they said unto me:
"Let us go unto the house of the Lord."
Our feet are standing
Within your gates, O Jerusalem;
Jerusalem, that is built
As a city that is compact together;
Whither the tribes went up, even the tribes of the Lord,
As a testimony unto Israel,
To give thanks unto the name of the Lord.
For there were set thrones for judgment,
The thrones of the house of David.

Pray for the peace of Jerusalem;
May they prosper that love you.
Peace be within your walls,
And prosperity within your palaces.
For my brethren and companions' sakes,
I will now say: "Peace be within you."
For the sake of the house of the Lord our God
I will seek your good.[3]

[2] *Ibid.* 87.
[3] *Ibid.* 122.

Long after the fall of Jerusalem, song and prayer kept the city alive in the minds and hearts of the Jewish people. During the three Pilgrimage Festivals, Pesaḥ, Shavuot, and Sukkot, there were always Jews who gathered in the city on the site of the ruined Temple to celebrate with prayer instead of sacrifice. Masses of Jews still flock to the Western Wall to celebrate the Festivals.

After the destruction of the Second Temple, many Jews hoped to restore it through prayer and penance by living ascetically, refusing to be comforted, and accepting a strict regimen of worship. These "mourners for Zion," as they were called, strove to arouse God's mercies for Jerusalem. They could be found in Jerusalem and in the Diaspora not only in the first centuries after the destruction, but throughout Jewish history.

This devotion is mirrored in the following passages from the Apocrypha: [4]

I lifted up my eyes and saw a woman at my right, and behold she was weeping and wailing aloud, and was deeply grieved; her clothes were torn and she had ashes on her head. I dismissed the thoughts I had been thinking, turned to her and said, "Why do you weep, and why are you grieved?"

She answered me, "Let me weep over myself, my lord, and continue to mourn, for I am greatly embittered in spirit and deeply afflicted."

I said to her, "What has happened to you? Tell me." She replied, "Your servant was barren and had no child, though I had a husband for thirty years. And every day and hour, those thirty years, I prayed to the Most High, night and day. Then after thirty years it came about that God heard your servant, looked on my affliction, gave heed to my distress, and granted me a son. I rejoiced greatly . . . and brought him up with great care. When he was grown up, I proceeded to take a wife for him, and made a marriage feast.

When my son entered his wedding chamber, he fell down and died. We all put out the lights, my neighbors rose up to comfort

[4] The Apocrypha is a corpus of Jewish religious writings originally written in Hebrew or Aramaic that date from the last centuries B.C.E. They were not included in the official Hebrew Bible which was canonized by the Rabbis of this period. These books, however, form part of the Greek Bible (Septuagint). See pp. 48–50 for another selection.

me and I was dumbstruck until the evening of the second day. When they stopped coming to comfort me I arose at night and fled to this field. I intend not to return to the city, but to remain here, I will neither eat nor drink, but mourn and fast continually until I die."

I interrupted my thoughts and said to her angrily:

"You most foolish woman, can you not see our sorrow, and what has happened to us? For Zion, our mother, is afflicted with grief and in deep humiliation. Now lament bitterly, for we are all lamenting, and be sad, for we are all sad, but you sorrow for just one son while we sorrow for the whole world. . . . Let yourself be persuaded because of the misfortunes of Zion, and be comforted because of the sorrow of Jerusalem. For you see that our sanctuary has been laid waste, our altar torn down, our temple destroyed, our harp is brought low, our song is silenced, our rejoicing has ceased, the light of our lamp is extinguished, the ark of our covenant is plundered, our sacred things are polluted, the name by which we have been called is profaned, our children are abused, our priests are burned, our Levites are gone into captivity, our girls are defiled, our wives are ravished, our righteous men are departed, our children are exposed, our young men are enslaved, and our strong men are weakened. Worst of all—Zion is now sealed up from her glory and delivered into the hands of our enemies. . . . "

It came to pass as I spoke to her, that her face suddenly shone and flashed like lightning. I was too frightened to go near her and wondered what it meant. Behold, she suddenly gave such a loud and fearful shriek the earth shook. I looked and behold the woman was no longer before me, instead, a city was being built, a place of magnificent foundations was revealed. I cried aloud.

[The angel Uriel said] . . . The Most High has seen righteousness, and your continual sorrow and lament over Zion. This then is the meaning of the vision: The woman who appeared to you . . . is Zion! As for her telling you that she was barren for thirty years, that was because for three thousand years there were no sacrifices offered in her; after three thousand years Solomon built the city, it was then that she bore a son. Her telling you that she brought him up with care, that was the period of residence in Jerusalem. Her saying to you, "When my son entered his wedding chamber, he fell down and died," and that misfortune overtook her, that was the fall of Jerusalem that occurred. . . . Now the Most High seeing your deep grief, and whole-hearted distress, has shown you the splendor of her glory and the charm of her beauty.[5]

Other passages from the Apocrypha reveal the continuing centrality of Jerusalem in Jewish thought.

> Then Tobit wrote a prayer of thanksgiving . . .
> Let all men speak of His greatness
> And give Him thanks in Jerusalem.
> O Jerusalem, the holy city,
> He will punish you for the actions of your children,
> But again will have mercy on the sons of the righteous.
> Give thanks to the Lord in goodness,
> And bless the King of Ages.
> That His tent may be rebuilt in you with joy. . . .
> Let me bless God, the mighty King,
> For Jerusalem will be built of sapphire and emerald.
> Her walls of precious stones,
> Her towers and fortresses of pure gold.
> The streets of Jerusalem will be paved with beryl,
>   ruby, and stones of ophir.
> Her lanes shall shout, "Hallelujah," and shall
> exclaim the praise, "Praised be God; who has
> raised you up forever." [6]

As the women living in Zion have just seen your exile,
They will soon witness your redemption by God . . .
Take courage, Jerusalem,
For He who named you will comfort you . . .
O Jerusalem, look eastward
And see the joy that comes to you from God,
Your sons are returning, whom you sent off.
At the command of the Holy One, they are gathered from
    east to west,
Rejoicing in the glory of God.
Jerusalem, remove your clothes of sorrow and affliction.
Put on the beauty of glory that comes from God forever.

[5] 2 Ezra, chaps. 9–10.
[6] Tob., chap. 13. This book is a moralistic tale probably composed at the beginning of the second century B.C.E.

Robe yourself in the cloak of righteousness from God,
Set the diadem of the Everlasting upon your head,
For God will demonstrate your splendor to all under heaven.
Your name shall be called by God forever:
"The Peace of Righteousness" and "The Glory of Godliness." [7]

It is the Jewish liturgy, however, that has most consistently and tenaciously impressed Jerusalem upon the Jewish spirit. Even in our own day, many regularly repeated songs of prayer and petition, celebration and gratitude, suggest Jerusalem—either in its past magnificence or its future majesty. Every Jew who performs the required modicum of worship, whether at home or in a congregation of fellow Jews, utters Jerusalem's name several times each day in the course of the service. The very pattern and order of Jewish worship are fashioned according to the ancient rites of the Temple service so that, consciously or unconsciously, the act of worship unites the Jew, beyond time and space, with the Temple of Jerusalem.

Although an individual Jew may have been hard put to locate Jerusalem on a map, the city was, nonetheless, an entity as real and as immediate to him as his own being. It was no less a mitzvah for him to remember Jerusalem than it was to keep the Sabbath or love his neighbor.

The Jew still chants daily at his table the most familiar lines in Jewish literature.

> If I forget thee, O Jerusalem,
> Let my right hand forget her cunning.
> Let my tongue cleave to the roof of my mouth.
> If I remember thee not;
> If I set not Jerusalem
> Above my chiefest joy.

These verses are from Psalm 137, which begins:

> By the rivers of Babylon
> There we sat down, yea, we wept,
> When we remembered Zion.

[7] Baruch, chaps. 4–5. This book comprises a text allegedly sent by Baruch, Jeremiah's secretary, from Babylonia to Jerusalem.

Upon the willows in the midst thereof
We hung up our harps.
For there they that led us captive asked
    of us words of song.
And our tormentors asked of us mirth:
"Sing us one of the songs of Zion."
How shall we sing the Lord's song
In a foreign land?

Jerusalem also figures in the blessing recited after every meal in which bread is eaten.

Have mercy, O Lord our God, upon Israel
Your people, upon Jerusalem Your city,
Upon Zion the abiding place of Your glory,
Upon the kingdom of the house of David.

Then this is added:

Rebuild Jerusalem the holy city speedily in our days. Praised are You, O Lord, who in Your compassion rebuilds Jerusalem.

On Sabbaths, Festivals and other special occasions, Jews recite the familiar verses from Psalms 126:

When the Lord brought back those that returned to Zion,
We were like unto them that dream.
Then was our mouth filled with laughter,
And our tongue with singing;
Then said they among the nations:
"The Lord has done great things with these."
The Lord has done great things with us;
We rejoice.

Turn our captivity, O Lord,
As the streams in the dry land.
They that sow in tears
Shall reap in joy.

Three times daily, except on Sabbaths and Festivals, the devout Jew supplicates God to return and rebuild Jerusalem.

Return in mercy to Your city Jerusalem and dwell in it as You have promised; rebuild it soon, in our days, as an everlasting structure, and speedily establish the throne of David in it. Praised are You, O Lord, Builder of Jerusalem.

Every prayer service includes the following:

May our eyes behold Your return in mercy to Zion. Praised are You, O Lord, who restores Your Divine Presence to Zion.

And every Kedushah concludes:

> And in Your holy Scriptures it is written:
> The Lord shall reign forever
> Your God, O Zion, for all generations,
> Hallelujah.[8]

The plea to rebuild the Temple is heard throughout the services —as part of each Amidah and after the Torah readings on weekdays and Haftorah portions on Sabbaths and Festivals. Readings from the Psalms also constantly recur in the prayer book.[9]

Introductory prayers include the following:

> The Lord rebuilds Jerusalem;
> He gathers together the dispersed of Israel. . . .
> Praise the Lord, O Jerusalem;
> Praise your God, O Zion.
> For He has fortified your gates;
> He has blessed your children within you.
> He establishes peace within your borders;
> He fills you with the finest wheat.[10]

Further on the worshiper adds: "Praised be the Lord out of Zion, who dwells in Jerusalem," [11] and concludes this section:

> Deliverers shall ascend to Mount Zion
> To rule the hill country of Esau;
> And dominion shall be the Lord's.[12]

On Mondays and Thursdays special petitions are uttered. At one point, the worshiper quotes Daniel 9:16–18.

[8] Ps. 146:10.
[9] Selections of prayers are based on *Daily Prayer Book*. See Further Readings and compare with any standard prayer book.
[10] Ps. 147:2, 12–14.
[11] *Ibid.* 135:21.
[12] Obad. 21

O Lord, in accordance with all Your righteous deeds, let Your anger and Your fury turn away from Jerusalem Your city, Your holy mountain; for because of our sins, and our fathers' transgressions, Jerusalem and Your people are held in disgrace by all who surround us. Now therefore, our God, hearken to Your servant's plea and supplication, and cause Your face to shine upon Your desolate sanctuary, for Your sake, O Lord.

Listen, my God, and hear; open Your eyes and see our ruins, and the city upon which Your name is called.

From the evening service for Sabbaths and Festivals:

> Spread over us your shelter of peace: Praised are You, O Lord, who spreads the shelter of peace over us and over all Your people Israel and over Jerusalem.

For all congregants who are privileged to come up to the Torah during a Festival God's blessing is invoked that they "may live to celebrate Festivals in Jerusalem together with all of Israel."

On Sabbaths and Festivals, the Jew prays in the solemn Kedushah:

> From Your abode, our King, appear and rule over us, for we await You. Oh when will You reign over Zion? Speedily, in our days, do dwell there forever. May You be exalted and sanctified in Jerusalem Your city throughout all generations and to all eternity.

As the Sabbath terminates, before Havdalah, the worshiper quotes from Isaiah (51:3).

> The Lord shall comfort Zion;
> He shall comfort her ruins,
> He shall make her wilderness like Eden,
> Her desert like the Lord's garden;
> Joy and gladness shall be found in her,
> Thanksgiving and song.

Before retiring each evening, verses from Psalm 128 are read.

> Behold thus shall the man
> Who reveres the Lord be blessed
> May the Lord bless you from Zion;

> May you witness Jerusalem's welfare
> all the days of your life;
> May you see your children's children.
> Peace upon Israel!

Feast days and fast days in the Jewish calendar consistently laud and commemorate Jerusalem. The Temple ritual is recalled in detail. The Passover Seder and the Yom Kippur service conclude with the exhortation "Next year in Jerusalem." In recent times Shavuot, the Festival of the First Fruits, has become once again the holiday on which Jews come to Jerusalem for special pageants and festivities. Many rituals on Sukkot, such as parading with an etrog and lulav, link the Jew with the Temple service.

On Rosh Hashanah and Yom Kippur the following verses are added to the evening prayer:

> Lord, grant honor to Your people, glory to those who revere You, ... joy to Your land and gladness to Your city. . . .
> You shall reign over all whom You created, You, alone, on Mount Zion, the abode of Your majesty, in Jerusalem Your holy city, as it is written in Your holy Scriptures: "The Lord shall reign forever, your God, Zion, for all generations" (Psalms 146:10).

In the additional service on Rosh Hashanah the following verse is added:

> On that day a great *shofar* shall be sounded; those who were abandoned in Assyria and those who were cast off in Egypt shall come and worship the Lord on the holy mountain at Jerusalem.[13]

Yom Kippur services contain the following passages, some of which echo Psalms:

> Remember the people You acquired long ago,
>   the nation You ransomed to be Your
>   very own, and Mount Zion where You dwelled.
> Lord, recall the love of Jerusalem; never
>   forget the love of Zion.
>
> Lord, remember the day of Jerusalem's
>   destruction at the hands of the

[13] Isa. 27:13.

> Edomites who shouted "Destroy it,
> destroy it, to its foundations."

> Arise and have mercy on Zion for now is
> the time to favor her.

> Bring us to Your holy mountain and delight us in
> Your house of prayer as it is written: "I shall
> bring them to My holy mountain and delight them
> in My house of prayer; their offerings and sacri-
> fices shall be accepted on My altar; My temple
> shall be called a house of prayer for all people"
> (Isaiah 56:7).

The Yom Kippur service also contains many references to the High Priest, who officiated only on that solemn day in the Holy of Holies.

> Fortunate the eye who witnessed all this, at its
> mention we grieve.
> Fortunate the eye that saw our Temple amidst the
> happiness of our nation, we grieve at its mention.

As part of the additional service on Yom Kippur, a poem by Rabbi Meshullam ben Kalonymus is read. The poem presents the intricate details of the Temple service as it was performed by the High Priest. What follows is a direct quotation from *Mishnah Yoma* 6:2, which is integrated into his poem.

> When the priests and the people, who were standing
> in the Temple court, heard God's glorious and revered
> name explicitly uttered by the High Priest with holi-
> ness and purity, they fell on their knees, prostrated
> themselves and worshipped; they fell upon their faces
> and said: "Blessed be the name of His glorious
> Kingship forever."

On Ḥanukkah, which celebrates the rededication of the Temple by the Maccabees over two thousand years ago, the following is added to the "thanksgiving," which is part of the daily service:

> We thank You for the miracles, the liberation, the heroic deeds
> and triumphs, and for the battles, which You carried out for our
> forefathers in those days, at this time.

In the days of the Hasmonean, Mattathias, son of Yoḥanan the High Priest, when an evil Greek kingdom arose against Your people Israel to make them forget Your Torah and transgress Your laws, You mercifully stood by them in their time of distress. . . . You delivered the strong into the hands of the weak. . . . Thereupon Your children entered the shrine of Your Temple, cleansed the sanctuary, purified Your Temple, kindled lights in Your court and established these eight days of Ḥanukkah to thank and to praise You.

Passover has its own range of Jerusalem memories. In the familiar *Dayenu,* we read:

Had He brought us into *Eretz Yisrael* and not built the Chosen Sanctuary for us, it would suffice us.

How many manifold favors did the Omnipresent perform for us! . . . He brought us into *Eretz Yisrael* and built the Chosen Sanctuary so that we might atone for all our iniquities.

In accordance with the ruling by Rabbi Akiba (born about 50 c.e. and martyred about 132 c.e.) in the Mishnah, the following prayer is recited at the Seder:

Praised are You, Lord our God, King of the Universe, who liberated us and liberated our forefathers from Egypt, and have kept us alive to this night so that we might eat matzah and bitter herbs on it. So may You, Lord our God, sustain us that we may celebrate other festive seasons and holy days which will occur in peaceful times. May we enjoy the restoration of Your city and be joyous in Your worship, and there we will eat of the festal and paschal sacrifices whose blood shall be sprinkled on the wall of Your altar for goodwill. We will thank You with new song for our liberation and our redemption. Praised are You, Lord, who redeemed Israel. (Some versions read: "who redeems Israel.")

Following this each participant puts bitter herbs between two pieces of matzah and says:

To recall the Temple days, we do as Hillel [last century B.C.E. to first century C.E.] ordained: "Thus Hillel did when the Temple was still standing—he combined matzah and bitter herbs and ate them together in accordance with the Biblical verse, 'They shall eat it together with matzah and bitter herbs' " (Numbers 9:11).

After drinking the fourth cup of wine, the celebrant recites:

> We pray to You, have pity, Lord our God, on Israel Your peo-
> ple, on Jerusalem Your city, on Zion Your glorious dwelling place,
> and on Your temple. Restore Jerusalem, the city of the Holy One,
> speedily in our days and bring us to it. Help us rejoice in its up-
> building, that we may eat of its fruit and be sated with its produce,
> and praise You for them in holiness and purity.

Eastern Jews continue the Seder with a series of poems composed during the Middle Ages. The first was written by Joseph ben
Samuel Bonfils (*Tob Elem*), a French Biblical commentator and
poet who lived during the middle of the eleventh century. This is a
selection from a longer composition intended for the Sabbath preceding Passover:

> The Passover service has now been concluded
>   according to its rules, ordinances and customs.
> As we have been deemed worthy to perform it now,
>   so may we be worthy to observe it in the Temple.
> You, who dwell on high, raise up the innumerable
>   people [Israel]
> Hasten to lead us, the plants of Your vineyard,
>   again redeemed to Zion with joyous song.

Then all loudly exclaim the familiar: "Next year in Jerusalem."

Serving even more directly as remembrances of Jerusalem's fate
are the fast days of the Jewish cycle of the year (other than Yom
Kippur). The fast of the Ninth of Av annually commemorates the
destruction of Jerusalem and the Temple.[14] On this day the Jew is
dramatically transformed into a solitary mourner for Zion. Barefoot and seated on an overturned bench, he mournfully intones the
ancient strains of the Book of Lamentations supplemented by
dirges (*kinnot*) composed by authors of diverse centuries and
countries of origin. This fast marks the culmination of a three-week
period which commences with the fast of the seventeenth day of
Tammuz. On that day, the Bible states, the Babylonians breached
the walls of the besieged Jerusalem. The fast of the Tenth of Tevet
commemorates the onset of Jerusalem's siege.

[14] See above p. 66.

In the afternoon service of the Ninth of Av, the following is recited:

Comfort, Lord our God, the mourners of Zion, the
mourners of Jerusalem, and the city that is in
mourning, laid waste, despised and desolate. She
is in mourning because she is without her
children:
she is laid waste as to her homes,
she is despised in the downfall of her glory,
she is desolate through the loss of her inhabitants.
She sits with her head covered like a barren, childless woman.
Legions devoured her, idolaters possessed her, they slaughtered
Your people Israel and killed the followers of the Most High.
Therefore, Zion weeps bitterly, Jerusalem raises her voice.
How my heart grieves for the slain. You, O Lord,
consumed her with fire and by fire You are destined to rebuild
her, as it is written: "I will be to her, says the Lord, a
wall of fire round about, and I will be the glory in her
midst" (Zechariah 2:9).
Praised are You, O Lord, comforter of Zion and builder of
Jerusalem.

As a result of the changes wrought by the reunification of the city after the Six-Day War, the Movement for Torah Judaism in Jerusalem has published the following text to replace the one above:

Lord, our God, with abundant compassion and enduring kindness take pity upon us, upon Your people Israel, and upon Your
city Jerusalem which is being rebuilt upon its ruins, restored upon
its ravage, and resettled upon its desolation.

For her most saintly martyrs who were wantonly slaughtered,
for those of Your people who were murdered and for her sons
who gave their lives and spilled their blood for her sake, Zion
moans and wails: "My heart, my heart cries for the dead, my
recesses weep for the dead."

Over the city which You liberated from the hands of villainous
legions and gave to Your people as an inheritance and to the children of Jacob in perpetuity, spread Your shelter of peace as a
peaceful river in fulfillment of that which is written: "I will be

to her, says the Lord, a wall of fire round about, and I will be the glory in her midst."

Praised are You, O Lord, comforter of Zion and builder of Jerusalem.

During the Middle Ages, there was a great development of liturgical poets, whose religious poems and songs (*piyyutim*) helped inspire and perpetuate the perennial bond between the Jewish people and Jerusalem.

Eleazar Kallir (ha-Kallir) was one such prolific *paitan* (liturgical poet) whose poems are still recited in the synagogues during various festivals, especially the Ninth of Av. There is still controversy over many biographical details related to Kallir, although many scholars maintain that he lived during the sixth or seventh century. One example of his work follows.

READER: On this night my children weep and wail,
           On this night my Temple was destroyed, my palaces burnt,
           Let the whole house of Israel moan in my grief,
           Let them bewail the conflagration that the Lord has kindled.

CONGREGATION: On this night my children weep and wail.

READER: On this night let the afflicted Israel cry,
           For on this day she became forsaken,
           Was separated from her Father's house.
           When she left His house,
           The door was shut and she went into captivity where she was devoured by all.
           On the day she was sent forth by devouring fire
           Fire and coals went forth from the Lord.

CONGREGATION: On this night my children weep and wail.

READER: On this night the wheel of misfortunes brought disaster.
           My first and second Temples were destroyed.
           The backsliding daughter was made to drink bitter waters and her body swelled as an unfaithful woman.
           She was sent from His house so that she has forgotten all good.

> Greater is the hatred than the love He had loved
> her:
> Living as in perpetual widowhood like a forsaken
> woman,
> Zion says: "The Lord has abandoned me."
> CONGREGATION: On this night my children weep and wail.[15]

During the eleventh century a prayer was composed to be recited when visiting the Western Wall:

> We thank You, O Lord our God and God of our fathers who has kept us alive and granted us the privilege of coming to Your chosen sanctuary which You selected above all of Jacob's settlements for Your abiding affection, both while it was standing and now that it is in ruins. As we have been allowed to see it in ruins, so may we be deemed worthy to admire it after its restitution, when all of Israel's exiles will be gathered therein. . . . May it be Your will, O Lord our God and God of our fathers, to take pity on its ruins, have compassion on its woe, clear away its dust, purify it from defilement, restore and rebuild its desolate breeches, and return us to this glorious sacred site so that we may dwell there as in ancient days according to the verse, "Therefore thus says the Lord: I return to Jerusalem with compassion: My house shall be built in it, says the Lord of hosts . . . " (Zechariah 1:16). Praised are You, O Lord, most praiseworthy Lord.

Another section from the same prayer of thanksgiving to be offered at the Western Wall reads as follows:

> I thank You, my God, for having sustained me and granted me life and strength to arrive here and behold the site of Your holy Temple for whose restoration all the people of Israel pray, that they may rest in its shade and lie in its dust. I, a servant son of your maidservant, have been privileged to see what I yearned for, and adore the object of my prayers, namely, to stand in front of your holy Temple. Although it lies in ruins, Your holiness pervades it. The nations may have defiled it, but it remains chaste by virtue of Your presence and Your promise: although You deny it to us now, You have sworn to return us to it and rebuild it.

[15] Adapted from *The Authorized Kinnot for the Ninth of Av*, p. 36. See Further Readings.

May it be our will, O Lord, our God, and God of our fathers, that You select me among those chosen to behold the fulfillment of Your promises.[16]

Solomon ibn Gabirol, one of the foremost poet-philosophers of the Golden Age of Spanish Jewry, was born in Malaga, in southern Spain, about 1022. In addition to composing poetry he engaged in Biblical exegesis and Hebrew grammar and wrote in Arabic several major works on philosophy and ethics which were subsequently translated into Latin (under the names Avencebrol, Avicembron, and Avicebron), with few recognizing their true author. His religious poems became integral parts of many Jewish rituals. He died sometime during the sixth decade of the eleventh century.

The following is from a hymn for the third Sabbath after Passover:

> The despoiled and dispersed Thou shalt gather to Zion,
> Restoring the slaves who were sold without fee,
> And the priests to their ritual robes, while the scion
> Of families ruling shall once more be free
> To carol, high God, his thanksgiving to Thee.[17]

In a hymn for the fourth Sabbath after Passover God says:

> Though bereaved and in mourning, why sit thus in tears?
> Shall your spirit surrender its hopes to its fears?
> Though the end has been long and no light yet appears,
>   Hope on, hapless one, a while longer.
> I will send you an angel My path to prepare,
> On the brow of Mount Zion your king to declare,
> The Lord ever regnant shall reign again there,
>   Your king, proclaim, comes to Zion.[18]

Another poet was Moses ben Jacob ibn Ezra, born in Granada, Spain, about 1055 to 1060. The early part of his literary career was devoted to poetry, whereas the latter part of his life was given almost entirely to philosophy. Compelled to flee from Granada, he

---

[16] Menachem Cohen, *Ha'Kotel Ha'Maravi* (Ramat Gan, Israel: Massada Ltd., 1968), pp. 93–94. My translation.

[17] *Selected Religious Poems of Solomon ibn Gabirol,* trans. Israel Zangwill (Philadelphia: Jewish Publication Society of America, 1923), p. 20.

[18] *Ibid.,* p. 22.

resided briefly in Christian Castile and subsequently spent most of his life wandering to strange cities. His large number of liturgical poems soon became part of various rituals, and his nonliturgical poems and his Arabic work on poesy were widely read.

> Have hope, O you that are so sore distressed,
> For He arises to put on retribution,
> And wrath does He don, as a turban,
> Rampart and wall He will restore,
> He will bind up the wounds of wandering and exile . . .
> The kings of the isles, who oppressed you with rigor
> Shall come with gifts, to behold your glory;
> And the nations shall walk in union by your light
> When my God rebuilds the city on the hill,
> With precious stones will He mark my borders.[19]

Judah Halevi (*ca.* 1085–1140) is the most famous of the Spanish Hebrew poets. His poetry, like that of most Hebrew authors of the period, was written for synagogal purposes. He also wrote drinking songs, poems of friendship, eulogies, and elegies.

"Zion, will you not ask if peace be with your captives?" is perhaps the most famous of Halevi's many Zionides. It is chanted each year as part of the Tishah Be'av service and has been rendered over sixty times into nine languages by Jews and non-Jews.

> Zion, will you not ask if peace be with your captives
> That seek your peace—that are the remnant of your flocks?
> From west and east, from north and south—the greeting
> "Peace" from far and near, take from every side.
> And greeting from the captive of desire, giving his tears like dew
> Of Hermon, and longing to let them fall upon your hills.
> To wail for your affliction I am like the jackals; but when I dream
> Of the return of your captivity, I am a harp for your songs. . . .
>
> Would I might be wandering in the places where
> God was revealed unto your seers and messengers.
> O who will make me wings, that I may fly afar,
> And lay the ruins of my cleft heart among your broken cliffs?
> I would fall, with my face upon your earth and take delight

[19] *Selected Poems of Moses ibn Ezra,* trans. Solomon Solis-Cohen (Philadelphia: Jewish Publication Society of America, 1934), pp. 99–100.

In your stones and be tender to your dust. . . .
The life of souls is the air of your land: and of pure myrrh
The grains of your dust, and honey from the comb your rivers.
Sweet would it be to my soul to walk naked and barefoot
Upon the desolate ruins where your holiest dwellings were. . . .
Zion, perfect in beauty! love and grace you did bend on to you
Of olden time: and still the souls of your companions are bound
up with you. . . .
Your God has desired you for a dwelling place, and happy is the
man
Whom he chooses and brings near that he may rest within your
courts.[20]

Another of Halevi's odes to Zion is even more ecstatic.

Beautiful of elevation! Joy of the world! City of the Great King!
For you my soul is longing from limits of the west.
The tumult of my tenderness is stirred when I remember
The glory of old that is departed—your habitation which is des-
olate.
O that I might fly on eagle's wings,
That I might water your dust with my tears until they mingle
together:
I have sought you, even though your King be not in you and
though, in place
Of your Gilead's balm, are now the fiery serpent and the scorpion.
Shall I not be tender to your stones and kiss them,
And the taste of your soil be sweeter than honey to me? [21]

Another poet, Abraham ibn Ezra (1092–1167), is the author of
a dirge recited on Tishah Be'av.

CONGREGATION: How much longer shall there be weeping in Zion
and mourning in Jerusalem?
O have mercy upon Zion and rebuild the walls of
Jerusalem.

READER: At that time, the Sanctuary was destroyed because
of our sins, and because of our iniquities our
Temple was burnt down;

[20] *Selected Poems of Jehudah Halevi*, trans. Nina Salaman (Philadelphia:
Jewish Publication Society of America, 1924), pp. 3–7.
[21] *Ibid.,* p. 19.

The heavenly Sanctuary which was bound firmly
with Jerusalem on earth joined in mourning
and the heavenly hosts raised a lamentation:

CONGREGATION: How much longer shall there be weeping in Zion
and mourning in Jerusalem?

READER: Not only did the tribes of Jacob weep bitterly,
but also the very planets shed tears. The stan-
dards of Jeshurun covered their heads in shame
and the Pleiades and Orion grew dim. . . .

CONGREGATION: How much longer shall there be weeping in Zion
and mourning in Jerusalem?

READER: Stir yourself for Zion with great zeal, and cause
your bright light to shine upon the city that
was so populous.

CONGREGATION O have mercy upon Zion and rebuild the walls of
AND READER: Jerusalem.[22]

An anonymous dirge strikes the same note of lamentation and
renewed hope.

A fire of joy is kindled within me as I think
of the time when I departed from Egypt.
But I will raise my lamentations, as I recall
the time when I departed from Jerusalem. . . .
Sabbaths and Festivals I enjoyed, signs and wonders
I witnessed when I departed from Egypt.
But fasting and mourning and the pursuit of vanity
were my lot when I departed from Jerusalem.
The Torah, the Testimony and the Order of the
Temple service were taught to me when I departed
from Egypt.
May I obtain gladness and joy, and let sorrow
and sighing flee away when I return to Jerusalem.[23]

The centuries passed, but *kinnot* continued to be written. An
example is the following dirge composed during the latter half of
the sixteenth century:

O Zion, lament for your house that is burnt.
Cry out in bitterness for the devastation of your vines. . . .

---

[22] *The Authorized Kinnot,* pp. 38–39.
[23] *Ibid.,* pp. 144–45.

They hunted you as though you were a bird,
There was none to help you
Against them when they spread their nets to reveal
    your shame. . . .
When Sarah hears your voice she, too, will cry for her
    children that were led captive among all your neighbors.
Weep, Rachel and Leah, protest with your presence and cry
    aloud. . . .
For God, who is everlasting, will surely not forsake you,
Zion, for there is hope of peace in abundance for your
    children.[24]

During the sixteenth century, too, the familiar Sabbath hymns, *zemirot,* were composed by various poets. They continue to be sung at dinner tables on Friday evenings and Saturday noon. Many contain references to Jerusalem.

Among these was *Yah Ribbon,* an Aramaic poem, a rhymed acrostic, composed by Rabbi Israel Najara, the author of a popular volume of songs entitled *Zemirot Yisrael,* which had widespread circulation among Jewish communities, particularly those in the Orient.

The last stanza reads:

> Return to Your most holy shrine,
> The place where all souls will rejoice
> And sing melodic hymns of praise—
> Jerusalem, city of beauty.[25]

Another popular Sabbath song is *Tzur Mishelo,* an anonymous hymn.

> Our God, O have mercy on Your people
> On Zion, Your shrine and our splendid home.
> May David's scion come to redeem us,
> The Lord's anointed, the breath of our life.
> Let the shrine be restored, Zion refilled
> That we may come up singing a new song
> Praised be the Merciful, Holy One
> Over the brimful cup of wine, God's gift.[26]

---

24 *Ibid.,* pp. 157–58.
25 *Daily Prayer Book,* p. 296.
26 *Ibid.,* p. 298.

Longing for redemption is a persistent theme in Jewish life. This explains, at least in part, why false Messiahs were able to excite the Jewish people; they zealously welcomed these messengers of deliverance, who sparked their imaginations with promises to liberate Jerusalem from the hands of the heathen. But each time the latest "messiah" was revealed as fraudulent and treacherous, a new wave of frustration and chagrin shook the Jewish communities. This extreme gullibility only serves to emphasize the hold of Jerusalem on Jews in every generation.

With the advent and dissemination of the *Zohar* and later of the specific form of Kabbalah mysticism taught by Isaac Luria (1534–1572), great stress was laid on *Tikkun,* or restoration. A complicated theosophy was developed, accompanied by mystical meditation. The emphasis was placed upon the individual worshiper, who, according to this teaching, could wield great powers for setting the world aright. By his prayers and religious practices the individual Jew might affect the coming of the Messiah. Everything a man did or said was of cosmic significance. As a direct result of such doctrines, there arose the custom, which eventually became very widespread, of *Tikkun Ḥatzot* (Midnight Prayer). As far back as the Talmud, midnight was considered a particularly propitious hour for prayer. The Kabbalists from the sixteenth century on reserved this time for special supplications dedicated to the redemption of Zion. This service, which was intended to influence the cosmic processes holding back the final, inevitable *Tikkun,* endowed the individual Jew with the power to bring about what his people had been striving for over the centuries.

This yearning is expressed in the *Lekha Dodi* chant with which Jews throughout the world welcome the Sabbath Queen every Friday evening. The hymn was composed by R. Solomon Alkabets, a Kabbalist who lived in Safed during the middle of the sixteenth century.

> Shrine of the King, royal city, arise
> Come forth from your ruins
> Long enough have you dwelt in the vale of tears
> He will show you abundant mercy.

Shake off your dust, arise
Put on your glorious garment
My people and pray: "Be near to my soul and redeem it
Through the son of Jesse the Bethlehemite!"

Bestir yourself, bestir yourself, for your light has come.
Arise and shine,
Awake, awake, utter a song
The Lord's glory is revealed upon you.

Be not ashamed nor confounded,
Why are you downcast? Why do you moan?
The afflicted of My people will be sheltered within you;
The city shall be rebuilt on its ancient site.

Those who despoiled you shall become a spoil
All who would devour you shall be far away
Your God will rejoice over you
As a bridegroom over his bride.[27]

[27] *Ibid.,* p. 246.

Chapter Five

TRAVEL LITERATURE

For so populous are the Jews that no one country can hold them, and therefore they settle in very many of the most prosperous countries in Europe and Asia both in the islands and on the mainland, and while they hold the Holy City where stands the sacred Temple of the most high God to be their mother city, yet those which are theirs by inheritance from their fathers, grandfathers, and ancestors even farther back are in each case accounted by them to be their fatherland in which they were born and reared, while to some of them they have come at a time of their foundation as immigrants to the satisfaction of the founders.[1]

What Philo, the Alexandrian philosopher, wrote about Jerusalem at the beginning of the Common Era has come to express the feelings of Diaspora Jews everywhere. While living in many lands, they continue to remember Jerusalem. And whenever possible, they have, from earliest times, fulfilled their yearning to see the ancient city.

After the destruction of the Temple, in place of the three pilgrimages which in ancient times used to be made annually, pious Jews, according to certain scholars, made it their duty to visit Jerusalem at least three times during their lifetime. In the ninth century one such visitor was Aḥimaaz. His famous chronicle eulogizes a certain Rabbi Samuel, who brought up the coffins of his parents and the bones of his father's uncle Rabbi Hananeel for burial in Jerusalem. Rabbi Samuel also donated twenty-thousand drachmas for the poor and indigent of Jerusalem, for the scholars and preach-

[1] Philo, trans. F. H. Colson, Loeb Classical Library (Cambridge, Mass.: Harvard University Press, 1962), vol. 9, *Flaccus,* pp. 327, 329.

ers who taught Torah, for the teachers and assistants, and for everybody at the Western Wall, as well as for the neighboring and outlying synagogues, and for the Temple mourners, for the students of Jerusalem's academies, and for the Babylonian academies.[2]

The medieval period saw the development of an extensive literature resulting from this widespread interest in travel to the holy city. Jerusalem was the subject of a large body of travelogues, memoirs, diaries, and correspondence. Many of these were objective, factual records of conditions in the city, while others were subjective and impressionistic.

At times the report was flavored by the reception afforded the visitor by the local Jewish authorities. For a balanced picture one must frequently rely on several separate accounts that complement each other.

The following letter, written at the end of the tenth century by the leaders of the impoverished Rabbanite community in Jerusalem, was addressed to their brethren in the Diaspora prior to a visit by their emissary, R. Jonah the Elder, for the purpose of gathering funds. It is the earliest of its kind. The entire letter is composed in rhymed verses, the first twenty-two of which form an alphabetical acrostic. Each verse is made up of five words, three of which begin with the same letter.

> Greetings to you from the faithful Lord, the eternal city and from the head of Zion's academies, from the city in which the seventy-one members of the Sanhedrin sat with their students before them . . . the city which now is widowed, orphaned, deserted, and impoverished with its few scholars. . . . Many competitors and rebels have arisen [referring to the Karaites] yet it yearns for the day its All-Merciful Lord will redeem it.
>
> We, the Rabbanite community, a pitiful assembly living in the vicinity of the Temple site, regret to inform you that we are constantly harassed by those foreigners who overrun the Temple grounds. We pray, "How long, O God, shall the adversary reproach? Shall the enemy blaspheme Your name for ever?" (Psalms 74:10). Our sole comfort will be when we are once again per-

---

[2] Aḥimaaz ben Paltiel, *The Chronicle of Aḥimaaz,* ed. and trans. Marcus Salzman (New York: Columbia University Press, 1924), p. 97.

mitted to walk freely about its gates, to prostrate ourselves in prayer for Jerusalem's total liberation with its Temple restored. . . . Yes, there is a synagogue on Mount Olivet to which our Jewish confreres gather during the month of Tishri. There they weep upon its stones, roll in its dust, encircle its walls and pray.

It was God's will that we found favor with the Ishmaelite rulers. At the time of their invasion and conquest of Palestine from the Edomites, the Arabs came to Jerusalem and some Jews showed them the location of the Temple. This group of Jews has lived among them ever since. The Jews agreed to keep the site clear of refuse, in return for which they were granted the privilege of praying at its gates. They then also purchased Mount Olivet, where the *Shekhinah* is said to have rested, as we read in Ezekiel 11:23, "The glory of the Lord went up from the midst of the city and stood upon the mountain which is on the east side of the city." . . . Here we worship on holy days facing the Lord's Temple especially on *Hoshana Rabba*. We entreat the Lord's blessing for all of Israel wherever they might reside. All who remember Jerusalem and its scholars are mentioned in our prayers. . . . All who recall Jerusalem will merit a share in its joy. . . . Everyone can partake of it by supporting Jerusalem's residents. Life here is extremely hard, food is scarce, and opportunities for work very limited. Yet our wicked neighbors exact exorbitant taxes and other "fees." Were we not to pay them we would be denied the right to worship at Mount Olivet. . . . These intolerable levies and the necessary frequent bribes compel us to borrow money at high rates of interest in order to avoid imprisonment or expulsion.

Help us, aid us, save us, redeem us. It is for your benefit too, for we pray for your welfare.[3]

During the latter half of the twelfth century Petaḥia b. Jacob ha-Laban journeyed from Ratisbon to the East and traveled to Palestine via Poland, southern Russia, Armenia, Persia, and Babylon.

Rabbi Petaḥia then went to Jerusalem. The only Jew there is Rabbi Abraham, the dyer, and he pays a heavy tax to the king to be permitted to remain there. They showed him Mount Olivet, and he saw that the pavement was three cubits high, which is the

[3] Abraham Yaari, *Igroth Eretz Yisrael* (Tel Aviv: Gazit, 1943), pp. 47–53. My translation.

breadth thereof. There is also a beautiful palace which the Ishmaelites built in ancient times when Jerusalem was still in the hands
of the Ishmaelites. Then came worthless persons who brought to
the king of the Ishmaelites a slanderous report, saying: There is
an old man among us who knows the locality of the Temple and
the court. Then the king grew urgent with that old man until he
pointed it out. The king was a friend of the Jews and said: I will
build here a temple, and none but Jews shall pray therein. He
built the temple of marble stone, a beautiful structure consisting
of red, green, and variegated marble. Then came Gentiles and put
images in it, but they fell down. They then fixed the images in
the thickness of the wall, but in the Holy of Holies they could
not place any. The hospice where the poor are is on another side.
The ground is cleft, and is called Valley of the Son of Hinnom,
where their burial-place is.[4]

One of the most famous travelers of the twelfth century was
Benjamin of Tudela. Describing a journey spanning from 1160 to
1173, his travelogue still serves as a primary source for the history
of the countries he visited. Some of his impressions of Jerusalem
follow:

From there it is three parasangs to Jerusalem, which is a small
city, fortified by three walls. It is full of people whom the Mohammedans call Jacobites, Syrians, Greeks, Georgians and Franks,
and of people of all tongues. It contains a dyeing-house, for which
the Jews pay a small rent annually to the king, on condition that
besides the Jews no other dyers be allowed in Jerusalem. There
are about two hundred Jews who dwell under the Tower of David
in one corner of the city. The lower portion of the wall of the
Tower of David, to the extent of about ten cubits, is part of the
ancient foundation set up by our ancestors, the remaining portion
having been built by the Mohammedans. There is no structure in
the whole city stronger than the Tower of David. The city also
contains two buildings, from one of which—the hospital—there
issue forth four hundred knights; and therein all the sick who come
thither are lodged and cared for in life and in death. The other
building is called the Temple of Solomon; it is the place built by
Solomon the king of Israel. Three hundred knights are quartered
there, and issue therefrom every day for military exercise, besides

[4] E. N. Adler, ed., *Jewish Travellers*, pp. 88–89. See Further Readings.

those who come from the land of the Franks and the other parts of Christendom, having taken upon themselves to serve there a year or two until their vow is fulfilled. In Jerusalem is the great church called the Sepulchre, and here is the burial-place of Jesus, unto which the Christians make pilgrimages.

Jerusalem has four gates—the Gate of Abraham, the Gate of David, the Gate of Zion, and the Gate of Gushpat, which is the Gate of Jehoshaphat, facing our ancient Temple, now called Templum Domini. Upon the site of the sanctuary Omar ben al Khataab erected an edifice with a very large and magnificent cupola, into which the Gentiles do not bring any image or effigy, but they merely come there to pray. In front of this place is the Western Wall, which is one of the walls of the Holy of Holies. This is called the Gate of Mercy, and thither come all the Jews to pray. . . .

In front of Jerusalem is Mount Zion, on which there is no building, except a place of worship belonging to the Christians. Facing Jerusalem for a distance of three miles are the cemeteries belonging to the Israelites, who in days of old buried their dead in caves, and upon each sepulchre is a dated inscription, but the Christians destroy the sepulchres, employing the stones thereof in building their houses. These sepulchres reach as far as Zelzah in the territory of Benjamin. Around Jerusalem are high mountains.

On Mount Zion are the sepulchres of the House of David, and the sepulchres of the kings that ruled after him.[5]

From Benjamin's report we also learn that there were "Mourners of Zion" in Yemen and Germany during the twelfth century. He recorded the following from hearsay:

They [the Jews of Yemen] give the tithe of all they possess unto the scholars who sit in the house of learning, also to poor Israelites and to the recluses, who are the mourners of Zion and Jerusalem, and who do not eat meat nor taste wine, and sit clad in garments of black. They dwell in caves or underground houses, and fast each day with the exception of the Sabbaths and Festivals, and implore mercy of the Holy One, blessed be He, on account of the exile of Israel.[6]

[5] M. N. Adler, ed., *The Itinerary of Benjamin of Tudela* (New York: Philipp Feldheim, 1964), pp. 22–24.
[6] *Ibid.*, p. 48.

Another traveler was R. Samuel ben Samson, who traveled to Palestine in 1210 in the company of the famous R. Jonathan ha-Cohen. At the end of his account, Samuel reports that he received a letter from John du Brienne, "king of Jerusalem," urging Jews to migrate to Jerusalem. Some historians hold that this letter may have prompted the famous pilgrimage of three hundred French and English rabbis in 1211.

We arrived at Jerusalem by the western end of the city, rending our garments on beholding it, as it has been ordained we should do. It was a moment of tenderest emotion, and we wept bitterly, the great priest of Lunel [Rabbi Jonathan] and I.

We entered by the [western] gate . . . as far as the Tower of David, whence it is customary to proceed for prostration before the approach to the Temple. We fell on our faces before the She-chem Gate, beyond which is the road which leads to the fount of Etham, the bathing place of the priests.

The gate opposite is in the western wall. At the base of this wall there is to be observed a kind of arch placed at the base of the Temple. It is by a subterranean passage that the priests reach the fount of Etham, the spot where the baths were.

From there we went to Mount Olivet, where in olden times the red heifer was burnt. We said our prayers there twice with a *minyan* [ten persons] and climbed the mountain. On the Sabbath day we recited the Afternoon Prayer on the spot where the un-circumcised had time and again set up a sanctuary with idols, whose presence the place would not endure, causing them to fall down again as fast as they were set up. It was one of the ten stations visited by the Divine Majesty when He came [to earth] from His dwelling place. The Ishmaelites venerate this spot. Only the foundations remain now in existence, but the place where the Ark stood is still to be seen.[7]

R. Moses b. Naḥman (also known as Naḥmanides or Rambam), a Spanish physician renowned for his work in Biblical exegesis, was compelled to leave his home in Barcelona and flee to Jerusalem. In a letter to his son, he described conditions in Jerusalem after the Tatar pillage of the city, which had occurred seven years prior to his visit.

[7] E. N. Adler, *Jewish Travellers*, pp. 103–4.

I write you this letter from Jerusalem, the holy city, for, thank
God, I arrived safely in Jerusalem on the ninth of Elul and shall
remain there till the day after Yom Kippur, at which time I intend to visit Hebron, where our forefathers are buried in order to
pray at their graves and prepare a burial site for myself. What
shall I relate about the conditions in the land? There is large-scale
destruction and ruin; in sum, the holier the site the more severe
the damage. Jerusalem is the most decimated of all the cities in
Palestine, and Judah is more blighted than the Galilee. Nevertheless, Jerusalem is very fine; its inhabitants number almost two
thousand of whom three hundred are Christians, refugees from the
ruler's sword. The Jews fled from the Tatars or were killed by
them, so that only two Jewish brothers, clothes-dyers, remain.
They purchase the exclusive right from the government, and a
minyan of Jews join them on Sabbaths. We encouraged them by
acquiring a destroyed house whose pillars and beautiful dome remained untouched, which we converted into a synagogue. We were
able to acquire it because the houses of the city were abandoned
and anyone who wished could claim them. We each donated funds
for its restitution, and we have dispatched messengers to Shechem
to return the Torah scrolls which were sent there from Jerusalem
for safe-keeping during the Tatar onslaught. A synagogue will be
erected and services conducted there, for many Jews continually
arrive from Damascus and Mesopotamia and the other regions of
Palestine. They come to see the Temple site and mourn over it.
May He who has granted us to see Jerusalem in its ruin, allow
us to witness its restoration and restitution when the *Shekhinah*
shall return to its midst. May you, my son, and your brothers and
all my household be permitted to see the good of Jerusalem and
Zion's comfort.[8]

The Holy City is described by still another traveler, Isaac ben
Joseph ibn Chelo (1334) of Aragon, who enumerates its "seven
wonders."

The first of these is the Tower of David. . . . It is of very ancient
and very solid construction, and in the olden times the Jews used
to dwell round about it. Today there are no habitations in the
vicinity but, instead, so many fortifications as to make this ancient stronghold quite impregnable in our time.

8 Yaari, *Igroth Eretz Yisrael,* pp. 85–86.

The second is an ancient building called Solomon's Palace. In former days, when the uncircumcised were in possession, this building was appointed to receive the sick of the holy city; today a market of considerable importance is held there.

The third is the tomb of the prophetess Ḥuldah. This prophetess, to whom in the time of King Josiah, the Maker of Sacrifices, there went Ḥilkiah, Aḥikam, Akbor, Shaphan, and Asahiah, was the wife of Shallum, son of Tikvah, son of Ḥarḥas, Keeper of the Wardrobe, who dwelt in Jerusalem. There she was buried, too, as was narrated by the great author in the following words: "They allowed no sepulchre in Jerusalem except the tombs of the House of David and that of Ḥuldah, which have been there from the days of the earliest prophets."

The tomb of Ḥuldah the prophetess, on the summit of the Mount of Olives, is very beautifully built. But the sepulchres of the House of David which were on Mount Zion are no longer known today either to Jews or Muslims; for they are not the Tombs of the Kings. . . .

These latter sepulchres are the fourth of the wonders of the Holy City. They are . . . near the cave of Ben Sirach. They are of ancient and very massive construction, in form a masterpiece of sculpture. All the strangers who come to visit the Holy City say they have never seen anything so beautiful.

The fifth of the curiosities to be seen is the Palace of Queen Helena, who came to Jerusalem with King Monobaz and was adopted into the Jewish religion there. This palace is a fine building inhabited today by the Cadi and his councilors.

The sixth is the Gate of Mercy, near the Temple. Formerly there were two gates, the one for wedding parties, the other for mourners, as we are told in the Chapters [*Pirke*] of Rabbi Eliezer the Great, the German Kabbalist, blessed be his memory! These two gates have been buried in the earth for the fulfillment of the Scriptures.

Finally, the last remarkable thing in the Holy City is the Western Wall, of which we spoke above.

The Jewish community in Jerusalem, God be gracious to her! is quite numerous. It is composed of fathers of families from all parts of the world, principally from France. The leading men of the community, as well as the principal rabbis, come from the latter kingdom—among others Rabbi Ḥaim and Rabbi Joseph.

They live there in happiness and tranquility, each according to his condition and fortune, for the royal authority is just and great. May God re-establish her and raise her to the highest prosperity!

Among the different members of the holy congregation at Jerusalem are many who are engaged in handicrafts such as dyers, tailors, shoemakers, etc. Others carry on a rich commerce in all sorts of things, and have fine shops. Some are devoted to science, as medicine, astronomy, and mathematics. But the greater number of their learned men are working day and night at the study of the Holy Torah and of the true wisdom, which is the Kabbalah. These are maintained out of the coffers of the community, because the study of the Torah is their only calling.[9]

Estori Farḥi (Parḥi), who lived in Palestine for seven years from 1312, traveling throughout the country and carefully recording its geography, flora, and fauna, also displays his scholarship.

What we see at present still remaining of the ancient walls [of the sanctuary] are fragments of the structure on the Temple Mount. We can still distinguish the Gate of Shushan on the eastern side; it is blocked by large square stones. If we divide this wall into three parts, the above-mentioned gate forms a portion of the southeastern extremity. We further recognize the Gate Ḥulda to the south, and the Gate Kefinus to the west; but the Tadi Gate is not distinguishable, because this side is demolished. At the distance of a bow-shot from the blocked gate, we see in the wall two very tall gates, with an archway on the outside and always closed by two iron doors, which the Arabs and simple folk call the Gates of Mercy. Those may be the two gates, mentioned in Tractate *Soferim* (chap. 2), built by King Solomon, one of which was destined for bridegrooms and the other for mourners and those who were excommunicated. On Sabbaths residents of Jerusalem would assemble and ascend to the Temple Mount between these two gates. Today, the people say their prayers in front of these two gates. . . .

The tent, which was erected by David for the Holy Ark, is still in a vault south of Mount Moriah, and is generally called the Temple of David. In front of it, towards the northwest, is a place which beyond doubt belongs to Zion. It is very near the synagogue erected there and near the Jewish quarter. But what shall we do?

[9] E. N. Adler, *Jewish Travellers,* pp. 130–33.

The roads of Zion are in mourning, its streets desolate, and its
sites not to be determined with any degree of certainty. The town
is presently higher than Mount Moriah, because it has been so
frequently destroyed and rebuilt on the same site, so that remains
of old vaulted roofs are found under the houses, and serve as
foundations for more recent buildings.[10]

In the latter part of the fifteenth century another traveler,
Meshullam ben R. Menaḥem of Volterra, recorded some impressions of "holy" places in the immediate surroundings of Jerusalem.

Below the temple area, in the valley, somewhat to the south, is
the monument of Absalom. It is built of large stones round it
and made "punte de diamanti." It is very beautiful, like a high
tower surrounded by pillars, and the whole structure is of single
stones, even the pillars. Round the tower are many caves of saints
who are buried there to the south, and a little more to the south
is the cave of the prophet Zechariah, may peace be with him,
and on the cave is a tower like Absalom's but the entrance to the
cave can be seen; and the cupola of the tower is in two parts,
and near the cave are many caves of saints buried there, and one
cave has a house built of a single stone. All who pass Absalom's
monument, even the Moslem, throw a stone on his grave because
he rebelled against his father, and at the side there is a very
great heap of stones, and every year the heap is removed.

On the southern side is Mount Zion, that is the city of David,
and above it, near to David's tomb, there is a church of the Fran-
ciscans. The place of David's burial is a house which has a great
iron door, and the Moslems take care of the key and honor the
place and pray there. Going down from there on the slope of
the hill is the Valley of the Son of Hinnom, which goes down to
the Valley of Jehoshaphat; and on the west is Millo, which is a
plain near the city where people go out to walk, especially the
Jews. On this road, if you go to the west about two miles, a little
distance from the road bed to the right on the way to Jerusalem
you find a cave with a door of hewn stone by which you enter.
It is all covered up and has many caves, cave upon cave, very
beautiful, those of the seventy Sanhedrin, and I prayed in that

[10] Translation from chapter 6 of *Kaftor va-Feraḥ,* based on the version in
A. Asher, ed. and trans., *The Itinerary of Benjamin of Tudela* (London,
1840–1), 2:397.

place; and if you go another two miles you come into a valley where there is a great bridge of stones, in which place David slew the Philistine. After that I ascended a big hill about two miles away, about six miles or a little more distance from Jerusalem, that is Ramah, the place of our lord the prophet Samuel, on whom be peace, and about half a mile before I reached Ramah I found two pools, that is, the upper pool and the lower pool. They are empty, and with no water, and when I ascended to Ramah at the top of the hill I saw a fortified town with high turrets in ruins, and the single house shut up which the Jews hold as a house of prayer, and the beadle of the synagogue, whose name is R. Moses bar Samuel, opened the door to me. It is beautiful and has a high vaulting, and I then entered a room which was as broad and big as the first, or a little less; and in that room there was a stone staircase going down to the cave, with a door also closed, and there is a synagogue in which a perpetual light is burning. Here is the tomb of our lord Samuel, the prophet, on whom be peace, and his father Elkanah, and his mother, Ḥannah, and his two sons. The Jews gather there every year and come even from Babylon, from Aram Zobah, which they call Aleppo, from Hamath, and from Gaza, and from Damascus, and Misr, and other places so that the foreigners by themselves are more than one thousand in number who come there every year on the 28th of the month of Iyar [11] to mourn and to pray in this cave; for on that day his soul was bound up in the bond of life, and all the Jews who come there are accustomed to buy oil to light in that synagogue, and I, poor man, prayed in that place and put oil there as is the custom, and I had a great and heavy burning ague when I prayed, and this was at the end of the month of July 1481. I also saw a bath of water under a small cave near to Ramah, about one-eighth of a mile away, which was the bath of the righteous Ḥannah, the mother of Samuel of Ramah; and when I returned to Jerusalem about a mile to the north I saw the grave of Simeon the Righteous in a cave, and all round Jerusalem there are many caves and in them are buried many pious and saintly people without number, but we do not know who they are except those marked; but it is a tradition amongst us from mouth to mouth from ancient times that there is no doubt as to their truth, and

[11] It is of interest to note that this is the exact date on which Israeli forces captured the Old City in 1967.

we see that the Moslems also honor all these places and that they have the same traditions about them as we. They ask the Jews, "Why do you not go to the grave of such a saint or such a prophet?" The Moslems have many a time sought to have these graves closed up and to have them dedicated as *wakuf* [12] in their hands, but God has opposed their intention and would not listen to them, for the Keeper of Israel neither sleeps nor slumbers. [13]

Obadiah Jaré b. Abraham, rabbi of Bertinoro, Italy, who is best known for his commentary which appears in almost every edition of the Mishnah, lived during the second half of the fifteenth century in Italy and died in Jerusalem at the beginning of the sixteenth century. Arriving in Jerusalem on March 25, 1488, he was immediately appointed head of the Jewish community. His erudition and reputation helped to invigorate the intellectual life of the Jerusalem community. He describes the living conditions in detail, in a document written in 1488.

About three-quarters of a mile from Jerusalem, at a place where the mountain is ascended by steps, we beheld the famous city of our delight, and here we rent our garments, as was our duty. A little farther on, the sanctuary, the desolate house of our splendor, became visible, and at the sight of it we again made rents in our garments. We came as far as the gates of Jerusalem, and on the 13th of Nissan, 5248, at noon, our feet stood within the gates of the city. Here we were met by an Ashkenazi who had been educated in Italy, Rabbi Jacob Calmann; he took me into his house, and I remained his guest during the whole time of the Passover. Jerusalem is for the most part desolate and in ruins. . . . Its inhabitants, I am told, number about four thousand families. As for Jews, about seventy families of the poorest class have remained; there is scarcely a family that is not in want of the commonest necessaries; one who has bread for a year is called rich. Among the Jewish population there are many aged, forsaken widows from Germany, Spain, Portugal and other countries, so that there are seven women to one man. . . .

The Jews are not persecuted by the Arabs in these parts. I have traveled through the country in its length and breadth, and none

[12] An Arabic word signifying an inalienable religious foundation.
[13] E. N. Adler, *Jewish Travellers*, pp. 189ff.

of them has put an obstacle in my way. They are very kind to strangers, particularly to anyone who does not know the language; and if they see many Jews together they are not annoyed by it. In my opinion, an intelligent man versed in political science might easily raise himself to be chief of the Jews as well as of the Arabs; for among all the inhabitants there is not a wise and sensible man who knows how to deal affably with his fellow men, all are ignorant misanthropes intent only on gain. . . .

The synagogue here is built on columns; it is long, narrow, and dark, the light entering only by the door. There is a fountain in the middle of it. In the court of the synagogue, quite close to it, stands a mosque. The court of the synagogue is very large, and contains many houses, all of them buildings devoted by the Ashkenazim to charitable purposes, and inhabited by Ashkenazi widows. There were formerly many courts in the Jewish streets belonging to these buildings, but the Elders sold them, so that not a single one remained. They could not, however, sell the buildings of the Ashkenazim, because they were exclusively for Ashkenazim, and no other poor had a right to them. The Jews' street and the houses are very large; some of them dwell also on Zion. At one time they had more houses, but these are now heaps of rubbish and cannot be rebuilt, for the law of the land is that a Jew may not rebuild his ruined house without permission, and the permission often costs more than the whole house is worth. The houses in Jerusalem are of stone, none of wood or plaster. . . .

Jerusalem, notwithstanding its destruction, still contains four very beautiful, long bazaars, such as I have never before seen, at the foot of Zion. They have all dome-shaped roofs, and contain wares of every kind. They are divided into different departments, the merchant bazaar, the spice bazaar, the vegetable market, and one in which cooked food and bread are sold. . . .

At present there is only one German rabbi here who was educated in Jerusalem. I have never seen his equal for humility and the fear of God; he weaves night and day when he is not occupied with his studies, and for six months he tasted no bread between Sabbath and Sabbath, his food consisting of raw turnips and the remains of the St. John's bread, which is very plentiful here, after the sugar has been taken out of it. . . .

All the necessaries of life, such as meat, wine, olives, and sesame-oil can be had very cheap. The soil is excellent, but it is not possible to gain a living by any branch of industry, unless it be that of a shoemaker, weaver, or goldsmith; even such artisans as these gain their livelihood with great difficulty. Persons of various nationalities are always to be found in Jerusalem from Christian countries, and from Babylonia and Abyssinia. The Arabs come frequently to offer up prayers at the temple, for they hold it in great veneration.

No Jew may enter the enclosure of the temple. Although sometimes the Arabs are anxious to admit carpenters and goldsmiths to perform work there, nobody will go in, for we have all been defiled [by touching bodies of the dead]. . . .

The Jews who come from Cairo to Jerusalem have only to pay ten silver denarii at the city gate, while, on the other hand, those who come by way of Jaffa have to pay a ducat. The Jews in Jerusalem have to pay down every year thirty-two silver pieces per head. The poor man, as well as the rich, has to pay this tribute as soon as he comes to the age of manhood.

Everyone is obliged to pay fifty ducats annually to the Niepo, i.e. the Governor of Jerusalem, for permission to make wine, a beverage which is an abomination to the Arabs. This is the whole amount of annual taxation to which the Jews are liable. But the Elders go so far in their iniquity that, in consequence of alleged deficits, they every week impose new taxes, making each one pay what they like; and whoever refuses is beaten by order of a non-Jewish tribunal until he submits.

As for me, so far God has helped me; they have demanded nothing from me as yet; how it may fare with me in the future I cannot tell. . . .

I have taken a house here close to the synagogue. The upper chamber of my dwelling is even in the wall of the synagogue. In the court where my house is there are five inhabitants, all of them women. There is only one blind man living here, and his wife attends on me. I must thank God, who has hitherto vouchsafed me His blessing, that I have not been sick, like others who came at the same time with me. Most of those who come to Jerusalem from foreign countries fall ill, owing to climatic changes and the sudden variations of the wind, now cold, now warm. All possible winds blow in Jerusalem. It is said that every wind before going where it lists comes to Jerusalem to prostrate itself before the Lord. Blessed be He that knows the truth.[14]

14 *Ibid.,* pp. 234ff.

In the seventeenth century, a guide book was published in Yiddish for travelers planning to go to the Holy Land. The author of *Darkhe Zion* was Moses Praeger, a scribe in Prague. It is filled with practical "dos" and "don'ts."

Many ways lead to Jerusalem. Every New Moon of Elul [late August or early September], many ships set out together from Constantinople, so one can proceed comfortably and also be secure, thank God, from pirates.

The caravan usually remains stationary by day and travels during the night on account of the great heat. The only bedding to take along is that which is to be used on the way. Feathers can be obtained cheaply at Jerusalem from the German community. You can never bring along a sufficient quantity of sheets, shirts, veils, tablecloths, handkerchiefs, and all other kinds of linen, for in Jerusalem these things are expensive and not very good. Each person should also take along a pair of good shoes as well as woolen winter stockings, for such clothing is not very good in Jerusalem. Apart from this, winter is cold in Jerusalem, even though it does not freeze. Men's clothing should not be brought along in quantity, for they are not expensive here. In Ofen let each man buy something to wrap around his head after the fashion of the Turks and if the cloth is quite white you should sew a few colored threads into it, but none of green. It is very dangerous to wear anything of green. Sometimes the borders of the prayer shawl are also green, and this must be changed in advance. Green, the color of the Prophet, is forbidden to Jews in the whole of Turkey and Jerusalem.

In Jerusalem many copper vessels are used and they are very expensive here. Let every man bring along his copper kneading basin, for bread is baked at home and the laundry is also washed there. One should bring copper pots, large and small, which have a tin lining inside. Also an iron tripod on which the pots are placed for cooking, likewise a pan for seething fish and a copper kettle for drawing water out of the cistern in each house. Also a basin which is taken along to the baths. The baths, thank God, are very good and healthful. Do not take much silver and gold along, even if you are rich, for that only attracts attention. But it is good to bring iron padlocks in order to lock up your rooms and boxes.

Books are not expensive in Jerusalem, so you should not burden yourself with them on account of the expense of transportation. Let each person take with him only a thick prayer book, a Pentateuch with commentaries, a Penitential Prayer Book, the Mishnah, Rabbi Mordecai Jaffe's *Levush,* a *Shomrim la-Boker,* a Festival Prayer Book according to the Prague usage, a Midrash, *En Yaakov,* the *Shulḥan Arukh,* and the *Yalkut.* The womenfolk take with them a *Teutsch Ḥumash,* Festival Prayer Book, and *Teḥinnah;* also other *Teutsch* books.

The prayer books should be small, for there is no lectern in the synagogues and the books must be held in the hand. A good housewife also will take Spanish sewing needles with her, also pins large and small, such as are needed and used at home.

All kinds of spices are to be found and very cheap; but muscat blossoms are rarely seen. Most foodstuffs are sold in Jerusalem by weight, and naturally other things as well. There is no beef, but now and again there is buffalo meat, which does not taste so good. Geese, ducks, chickens, and doves are found in plenty and cheap. There are two kinds of oil; one called *Siridj* is very cheap, better than goose fat or butter and is made of seed. The other oil is sweet oil, cheaper than *Siridj* but not so good and also not good for burning. Young radishes, all kinds of onions, and parsley root are all very cheap and can be had all the year round. Large citrons for preserving, oranges, and lemons, appear in the market all the winter. Sometimes oranges are eight for a kreutzer, and sometimes even cheaper. They are used to make lemonade, and folk keep the juice fresh in glasses by adding a little olive oil on top. Mushrooms or German chanterelles are very cheap. In winter there is fresh fish, both large and small, but different kinds from those to be found abroad. The fish are caught in the sea and brought here in a day and a half. That is why there is no fresh fish in summer; for it can go bad on the way.

For a large living room an annual rent of eight lion thalers is paid; for a smaller, five or six. Folk who dwell in the Synagogue Court, where the Loeb Synagogue and the two Houses of Study are, live cramped and often lack water. But on the other hand they can go to the synagogue very early in the morning every day. For the synagogue is locked in the evening as soon as the Evening Prayer is over, and not opened again until the break of day. To go through the streets at night is dangerous. Anyone who does not dwell in the Synagogue Court has ample room and also more water at home. The water is good and healthful. He who so desires can drink it with liquorice at twenty kreutzer the rotl. There are some who also drink it with lemonade. The water is only rain water and not well water.

Every house has a large, very well whitewashed cistern under the ground, and up above there is a little hole, where the water runs in and is drawn up. In years when there is little water it must be bought from Turks, who bring it into the house in leather sacks.[15]

The memoirs of a Jerusalemite during the years 1625–26 depict the agony of the Jewish residents under a hostile Turkish ruler, Pehah Muḥammad ibn Faroukh.

In the year 1625 under the Sultan Murad of Turkey Muḥammad Basha was governor of Jerusalem. The city of our God was then more greatly populated than at any time since the first exile because Jews constantly arrived to settle here. In addition pilgrims came to pray to "Him who stands behind our wall." . . . They would not come empty-handed. On the contrary, they gave freely for the support of the Jewish community in Jerusalem. Jerusalem's fame spread. It became known that we lived here in peace and tranquility. Many of us purchased homes and fields and rebuilt the ruins; our elders dwelt in the streets of Jerusalem, which were filled with children. From Zion, the fairest of all cities, the Lord appeared, for His teachings spread from its academies. The Torah and the word of God went forth from Zion to all the inhabitants of the world . . . many academies were opened and scholars flocked to their gates . . . and our wealthy brethren in the Diaspora supported them. . . .

One day, however, the most wicked and evil Muḥammad b. Faroukh, blind in one eye, came and entered Jerusalem with three hundred mercenary soldiers who proceeded to depose Muḥammad Basha. Immediately thereafter he set himself against us, and mercilessly tortured us and the Arab and Christian residents as well. Placing guards at the exits from the city, he ordered many to be brought bound and tortured before him so that he could extort and confiscate their money. . . . For two years we were persecuted, harassed, and molested so that many fled the city. . . . One year later the city was liberated by the troops of Ḥassan Basha . . . but one cannot recount the property losses and personal sufferings endured during those abominable days.[16]

[15] Reprinted by permission of Schocken Books Inc. from Kurt Wilhelm, ed., *Roads to Zion,* pp. 65 ff. Copyright © 1948 by Schocken Books Inc. See Further Readings.
[16] Abraham Yaari, ed., *Zikhronot Eretz Yisrael (1625–1938),* 2 vols. (Jerusalem: World Zionist Organization, 1947), 1:45–47. My translation.

Gedaliah of Siemiatyeze, author of *Sha'alu Shelom Yerusha-layim,* was a member of the group headed by Rabbi Judah Ḥasid, who left Poland in 1699 with more than 1300 disciples to live in Jerusalem. The rabbi died immediately after his arrival in Jerusalem, and his followers suffered many hardships.

In the late summer of the year, shortly before our arrival, a beginning was made at the building of the new synagogue and of forty dwellings for the poor. These buildings consumed a great deal of money. The Turks in Jerusalem had to be heavily bribed before they permitted the building. Then the Jews of Jerusalem wished to construct the new synagogue on a larger scale than the old one, but the Turkish government permitted them to build it only as high as the previous building. So then they had to bribe the pashas heavily again, in order that they might approve a larger building. . . .

Our debts press like a heavy yoke on our necks. We are continually taken into custody and before one debtor can be redeemed, another has already been detained. One scarcely dares to go out in the street, where to cap it all, the tax collectors lie in wait like wolves and lions to devour us. . . .

But now we are oppressed with debts, and we have to give the money meant for our sustenance to the Turks, so that they should not fling us into prison, for the prison is worst of all. . . .

The Arabs often wrong the Jews publicly. But if the Arab is a respectable man he will cause no injury to the Jew whom he meets in the street. The meeting with common people is often unpleasant for the Jews. We may not raise a hand against a Turk, nor against an Arab either, who has the same religion as the other. If one of them gives a Jew a blow, the Jew goes away cowering and does not dare to open his mouth, lest he receive worse blows.

That is the way the Sephardim behave who have grown accustomed to the situation. But the Ashkenazic Jews, for whom it is not yet customary to receive blows from Arabs, curse them if they know the language or leap upon them in fury, and then receive even more blows. But if a respectable Turk comes along, he scolds the Arab thoroughly and drives him away; or else he waits until the Jew has gone his way. The Christian must also suffer such indignities. If a Jew makes a Turk angry, then the latter beats him shamefully and dreadfully with his shoe, and nobody delivers the Jew from his hand. Nor is it otherwise with the Christians. They find themselves under the same oppression, but they have a great deal of money which is sent to them from all over, and they bribe the Turks with it and keep them away. The Jews do not have much money, and it is much worse for them.

Despite all the hardships, however, Gedaliah writes that "it is a rare delight to dwell in the Land of Israel, and 'he who walks only four ells in the Land of Israel has a share in the everlasting life.' "

When a scholar here goes to a place which he has never before visited, it is the custom for him to say: "I have gone a fresh four ells." Likewise the commandments which are only valid in the Land, as for example the provision that the priests shall be given the shoulder and the cheeks and the maw of all that is slaughtered, are still observed in the Land. Myself once slaughtered a lamb, and with God's aid I delivered his portion to a priest. We give heave-offerings and tithes of wine and brandy. One Friday I bought grapes in order to press out the juice for the Kiddush [Benediction of Sanctification] and then I was able to fulfill one commandment through fulfilling another—namely by giving a heave-offering and a tithe of the grapes. The prescriptions of the sabbatical year are likewise observed. The year before our arrival was such a sabbatical year. . . .

Here we have no other occupation than to study and to pray by day and night. And as a reward may the words of the prophet Isaiah be fulfilled for us all speedily and in our days: "And the ransomed of the Lord shall return, and come with singing unto Zion, and everlasting joy shall be upon their heads; they shall obtain gladness of joy, and sorrow and sighing shall flee away" (Isaiah 35:10).[17]

17 Wilhelm, *Roads to Zion*, pp. 73ff.

Chapter Six

NEW-OLD JERUSALEM

In the last decades of the nineteenth century the Zionist movement, whose very name connects it with Jerusalem and Zion, had already begun to capture the imagination of the Jewish people. This resurgence of Jewish nationalism kindled a renewed interest in Jewish cultural activities, which, in turn, gave fresh impetus and a much needed vitality to modern Hebrew and Yiddish literatures. Adapting Western literary modes, genres, and criteria, Jewish writers infused them with specifically Jewish accents and themes. As might be anticipated, their early efforts were sometimes naive and unsophisticated. It must be remembered, however, that these authors struggled against heavy odds. Their influence on later writers must also be acknowledged.

Nineteenth-century poetry and prose contain many references to Jerusalem. Indeed, a number of authors demonstrate a deep emotional attachment to Zion and a tendency to idealize Jerusalem. The first modern Hebrew novel, published in Vilna in 1853, bears the name *Ahavat Tziyyon* (Love of Zion). It contains many flowery passages in which the author, Abraham Mapu, relying mainly on Biblical references and without ever having seen Jerusalem, attempted to recreate the ancient city. A brief sample will suffice to convey its highly romanticized and sentimental tone.

"Behold!" cried Amnon. "The city is full of noise and bustle. How stately stand its palaces, while its towers, reaching to the clouds, resemble giants. The people in dense multitudes press through the streets. One man directs his steps here, another there, as he may be inclined, for purpose and desire are the angels who influence men's deeds. The ear perceives the bustle, but the understanding heart

143

pursues its own right way, for all the activity of the multitudes and their purpose and desire are worthless unless they are from the Lord. For as the Sanctuary on Mount Moriah is exalted above all palaces, so is the will of God above the will of those who dwell in houses of clay."

"Sing us," said Thamar, "one of thy songs of Zion, adapted to this spot from whence we can overlook the city with all its pomp." Amnon seized his harp, and sang:

> Jerusalem, the mighty
> Zion our gathering place,
> Jehovah hath thee chosen
> And shown to thee His grace.[1]

Another writer of this period, Mordecai Zeev Feierberg (1874–1899), is equally emotional in his modern quasi-autobiographical novel *Whither (L'An)*, which rapidly became a classic of Hebrew literature. The following is a description of a portion of the *ḥatzot* (midnight prayer) ritual in which the young hero, Naḥman, envisages return to Zion as the only salvation for Europe's Jews.

Naḥman recalls the many stories he has heard from Jews of the Holy Land, who tell about the walls of Jerusalem. He sees before him the Western Wall of the Temple. He stands amid the ruins near the holy wall. He sees a mass of Jews strewn on the ground, wailing aloud. Here are the remnants of the battered towers; from the ruins he hears a voice calling, "Woe unto the father who banished his sons; woe to the children who are banished from their father's household." A heavy veil darkens Jerusalem, the city is mourning. At the gate of the city, at the mouth of a cave, sits old King David, his lyre in his hand, and he chants a mournful song. Not far from the cave stands an armed Ishmaelite, his sword at his side, a spear in his hand. He is guarding the city. But, there, there far away, the heavens are opened, the Holy One blessed be He, sits upon His throne, and sees the earth at His feet. He sees Jerusalem in desolation. Then the throne of Heaven sweeps from its place in a whirlwind and two great hot tears fall into the depths of the sea. Then there go forth from Eden all those sanctified souls who have been slain for God's glory. Before them flows a river of blood, and about

[1] From a translation by B. A. M. Schapiro entitled *The Shepherd-Prince* (New York: Brookside Publishing Co., 1922), p. 138.

them flames shoot forth, their mangled bodies ripped into strips, their lean hands raised to Heaven, and among them bits of parchment from scrolls of the Law which they rescued from the foe, and they all prostrate themselves and fall before the Throne of Glory.

Then a fearful voice is heard from on high: "Return, ye purified souls, return to your rest, the end has not yet come." The matriarch Rachel cries out in a voice that melts the heart, before the Throne of Glory, and the sacred patriarchs prostrate themselves and cry with fearful agony. But the long bitter exile is not yet over; Jerusalem burned with fire, the Holy Land in desolation, the Divine Presence in exile, and Israel scattered among the nations of the earth. Satan has triumphed, Samael rules over all things, Michael the guardian of Israel [Father says] bound in chains. Desire rules over us, and we cannot serve the Lord. O, when will Messiah come? Messiah must come; we must bring him. Messiah will not come of himself [says Father], the generation must bring him. But have not many wanted to bring the Messiah? Joseph de la Reina? The Ashkenazi Rabbi Isaac? And the Baal Shem? They could not bring him, for the end did not come in their time. We must bring the Messiah, we must bring him, come what will!

The most glowing accounts of Jerusalem of this period are to be found in the memoirs of those Jews who fulfilled the sacred duty of pilgrimage, returning to Jerusalem with the same zeal displayed by their ancestors. In the tradition of ancient and medieval Jewry, modern Jews rarely failed to be deeply moved by the experience.

One of the most important of these "modern" pilgrims was Theodor Herzl, the father of political Zionism.

We arrived at Jerusalem under a full moon [October 29, 1898]. I would have gladly driven the half-hour's distance from the station to our hotel; but the gentlemen made such sour faces that I had to resign myself, down with fever as I was, to walking to the city. I literally tottered along on my cane. . . .

In spite of my weariness, Jerusalem and its grand moonlit contours made a deep impression on me. The silhouette of the fortress of Zion, the citadel of David—magnificent!

The streets were alive with Jews sauntering in the moonlight. I felt very sick before going off to sleep. . . .

In the morning I awoke relieved. But I am still very feeble. It is now evening, and I have not stirred from the house. All I can do is look out of the window and conclude that Jerusalem is magnificently situated. Even in its present decay it is a beautiful city; and, if we get in here, can become one of the finest in the world.[2]

Herzl's practical mind was quick to envision improvements in the Old City and the building of a New Jerusalem outside the walls.

Jerusalem, October 31, (1898).

When I remember thee in days to come, O Jerusalem, it will not be with delight.

The musty deposits of two thousand years of inhumanity, intolerance, and foulness lie in your reeking alleys. The one man who has been present here all this while, the lovable dreamer of Nazareth, has done nothing but help increase the hate.

If Jerusalem is ever ours, and if I were still able to do anything about it, I would begin by cleaning it up.

I would clear out everything that is not sacred, set up workers' houses beyond the city, empty and tear down the filthy rat-holes, burn all the non-sacred ruins, and put the bazaars elsewhere. Then, retaining as much of the old architectural style as possible, I would build an airy, comfortable, properly sewered, brand new city around the Holy Places. . . .

I am firmly convinced that a splendid New Jerusalem can be built outside the old city walls. The old Jerusalem would still remain Lourdes and Mecca and Yerushalayim. A very lovely beautiful town could arise at its side.[3]

I would cordon off the old city with its relics, and keep out out all ordinary traffic; only places of worship and philanthropic institutions would be allowed to remain inside the old ramparts. And on the ring of encircling hillsides, which our labor would clothe with greenery, there would gradually rise a glorious New Jerusalem. The elite from every part of the world would travel the road up to the Mount of Olives. Loving care can turn Jerusalem into a jewel.

[2] Reprinted from *The Diaries of Theodor Herzl*, ed. Marvin Lowenthal (New York: Dial Press, 1956), p. 283. Copyright © 1956 by The Dial Press, Inc. and used by permission of the publisher.
[3] *Ibid.*, pp. 283–85.

Everything holy enshrined within the old walls, everything new spreading round about it.[4]

In his memoirs, covering the period from 1855 to 1869, pioneer Josef Joel Rivlin provided a description of the actual settlement that developed outside the walls. The settlement was sponsored by Sir Moses Montefiore, the patron of Jerusalem, who in 1857 built houses with money bequeathed by the wealthy American Judah Touro. The houses were known both as the "Touro quarter" and the "Montefiore Homes." At the outset Montefiore had tried to set up first a textile factory and then a hospital, but neither succeeded. Even the decision to pay a number of poor families to live outside the walls was unsuccessful, and the homes remained vacant for several years. Fear of brigands, thieves, and raiders kept inhabitants inside the city walls. The city's gates were locked each evening, and even the Arabs were afraid to go beyond the walls in the daytime.

It was Josef Rivlin who refused to give up the idea of a New Jerusalem. He continued preaching its necessity in Ashkenazi and Sephardi synagogues. In 1857 he founded a society called "Builders of Jerusalem" and began to collect names of all interested parties. Some joined out of sympathy for him, others in anticipation of personal rewards.

> In 1859 Rivlin was invited by relatives to come to Shklov and Mogilev . . . he presented his idea and it captured their imagination. . . . Nine months later he returned and subsequently eight hundred roubles were collected and forwarded to him. . . . This was the money which enabled the society to buy the properties on which the first buildings were erected.[5]

Another account of early pioneer days describes the founding of Meah She'arim outside the city gates. This writer also laments the dilapidated state of Jerusalem and reaffirms the will to rebuild the city.

> In our age, as we observe Jerusalem's present condition, we note that what was true of the former returnees is repeated today. Our

4 *Ibid.*, p. 290.
5 From Rivlin's diary, in Abraham Yaari, ed., *Zikhronot Eretz Yisrael (1625–1938)*, 1:183–85. My translation.

happiness is tinged with sadness. Jews who come from the European Diaspora with its tumultuous cities know only too well that the city of the Lord has sunk to the lowest depths; they lament and bewail its ruins. While we, the residents of Zion, have known worse days, and yet we are no less grieved at Jerusalem's sorry state.

But now, as we observe the slow transformation, with the city shaking off its dust and donning a robe of majesty, we are thrilled and rejoice that the Lord's hand has wrought all this. We hope and trust that in like manner the Lord will lead us and not remove His hand from our midst, so that we may see our final liberation when the Lord shall comfort His people; then shall we see Zion's children restored within her borders dwelling in eternal bliss, with all of the prophets' visions fulfilled.

We therefore, the sacred community of Meah She'arim in Jerusalem, the holy city, may it speedily be restored, recognizing the graciousness of the Lord and His abiding goodness and conscious of our unique position, hereby lay the cornerstone, with which we begin the rebuilding of the abandoned sections of the holy city, Jerusalem, whose glory and pride will be restored as all the faithful can see. We, like our ancestors, proceed alone; with our own hands have we prepared all this.[6]

Menahem Ussiskin, another early Zionist, describes the deep emotions stirred in the returnees as they celebrated their first Passover on the hallowed soil.

Time and place converged to create for us an unprecedented, rhapsodically enchanting event. The location: Jerusalem, the sacred city. The word itself suffices to explain the sublime ecstasy that enveloped us: this is the ancient, divine city on which were embossed the valor and splendor of the glorious Jewish past! Here sat the kings of Judah, here Hebrew prophecy and wisdom blossomed. It is the joy and capital of the entire universe. Here, yes, in this very place lies before us our people's brilliant history. Will not its future be linked to this place?

The occasion: Passover even after the Seder—the night called "the watchful night," at which season the people of Israel had left their bondage for freedom, the festival commemorating the date on which our people became a nation. . . . These memories of our

6 *Sefer Ha-Taqqanoth, Le-Meah Shearim.* My translation.

former grandeur were evoked in each one of us. As we sat under the deep-blue skies studded with myriads of sparkling stars, each of us wished to pierce the clouds of history and return to that moment of freedom when a dynamic Jewish people inhabited this place and celebrated its holy days. Each of us was confident, too, that he was grasping not only the Jewish people's past but also its future. . . . For, truth to tell, ancient Israel was returning to its former homeland. . . . Every day tens and hundreds of Jews were gathering from the four corners of the earth with one goal: "to renew its days as of old."

All private conversations slowly came to a halt. Everyone felt that human speech was inadequate to express what was transpiring in the heart—at this sublime moment, silence was the most appropriate expression. . . . All at once, someone asked, as he pointed to the Temple Mount, "What will arise on that spot in the future when the Jewish people returns to its land?"

"A synagogue, a sanctuary," someone replied; "our synagogues are occupied by enemies and we will merely be reclaiming what is lawfully ours."

"Not at all," remarked a third. "We will not turn it into a sanctuary, nor into a chapel for worship and weeping. It will serve instead as a temple of wisdom and life; here will be housed the highest institute for the humanities. We have wept and prayed enough! The time has come to study and teach!"

"Indeed, the problem was resolved by the wisest of all men, King Solomon over three thousand years ago!" Aḥad Ha'am interjected quietly but firmly. Turning toward Mount Moriah, he recited with calm pride Solomon's prayer at the dedication of the Temple which he had erected to the God of Israel.

The young writer's voice which was soft at the outset grew stronger and stronger. The words of the king who had loved foreigners rang out in the silence of the night as a prophetic vision.

"Yes," Aḥad Ha'am reiterated, "there shall be erected a temple— that shall be neither synagogue, church, nor mosque, but rather a house of worship for all the peoples of the earth. . . ."

At that moment, each of us felt ecstatic. For a long time afterward we stood still as we pondered his statement, each of us felt as if a solution had been offered to one of humanity's most perplexing dilemmas.[7]

---

[7] Yaari, *Zikhronot Eretz Yisrael,* 2:696–98.

Among the numerous odes to Zion penned during this period of the return to Zion, one, *Hatikvah* (by Naftali Herz Imber), was the best known and has since been adopted as Israel's national anthem.

> So long as still within our breasts
>   the Jewish heart beats true;
> So long as still towards the East,
>   to Zion, looks the Jew,
> So long our hopes are not yet lost—
>   two thousand years we cherished them—
> To live in freedom in the land
>   of Zion and Jerusalem.

During the early decades of this period Jerusalem symbolized the Jews' former majesty, and this offered the returning pioneer-poets a wellspring of self-assurance. The associations attached to every corner of Jerusalem generated an extraordinary moral strength that enabled the Jews to endure defeat and hardship. In no way, then, had Jerusalem and the Wall lost their mysterious hold.

Put Me in the Breach

by Judah Karni

Put me in the breach with every rolling stone
    And set me fast with hammers
Perchance I may atone for my homeland, and the guilt
    Of the people who closed not up the waste places be forgiven.

How good to know that I am a stone like all the stones of Jerusalem,
    How happy were my bones bound up with the wall
Why should my body be poorer than my soul which in fire and water
    Accompanied the people in tears or silence?

Take me with the Jerusalem stone and set me in the walls
    And plaster me with lime

And from the breaches of the wall my failing bones
Would shout with joy to welcome the Messiah.[8]

Jerusalem

by Avigdor Hameiri

From the summit of Mount Scopus,
I bow me down before thee,
From the summit of Mount Scopus,
Jerusalem, I greet thee,
A hundred generations I have dreamt of thee,
Hoping once more thy face to see.

Jerusalem, Jerusalem,
Shine forth upon thy son!
Thy ruins, O Jerusalem,
I will rebuild, each one.

From the summit of Mount Scopus,
Jerusalem, I greet thee.
Thousands of exiles from afar.
Lift up their eyes to thee.
A thousand blessings we will sing,
City and Temple of our King.

Jerusalem, Jerusalem,
I will not stir from here!
Jerusalem, Jerusalem,
Come, O Messiah, come near! [9]

At Your Feet, Jerusalem

by Uri Zvi Greenberg

Kings cast wreaths at your feet and fall upon their faces
And they are then wonderful servants to you and your God.
Rome too sends its marble, crystal and gold
To build within you a summit sanctuary for fame and glory.

---

[8] Ruth Finer Mintz, ed. and trans., *Modern Hebrew Poetry* (Berkeley and Los Angeles: University of California Press, 1966), p. 108. Reprinted by permission of the Regents of the University of California.

[9] *Israel Youth Horizon* 3, no. 6 (April–May 1952): 19. Translator unlisted.

But we, but we your barefoot sons and daughters
  Who come to you beggared from the ends of the world,
We are, that which here we are, children
  Of the sovereign to the cactus growing by itself, to the
    waves of cliffs.
We who leave the Jewish community
  In the world, put our coat of many colors, like a lizard,
    into the bag.
Father scolded, mother wept, and the white bed was orphaned.
To you we have brought blood and fingers, love and muscles:
    unburdened
  Shoulders to carry the Hebrew globe with its open sores.
All our dreams and our ambitions we gave up
  That we might be poor laborers in the wasteland.
Where in the world can you find its like? Ask, you who were
    burned by Titus!
  Where do they love sullied sovereignty with eternal love?
Where is the wailing of jackals heard with great compassion?
  Where do they fever in red song, where do they shrivel
    and grow silent
And cool flaming foreheads and kiss the cliffs?
The heatwind here slowly burns away our dear youth
  Whose dust is scattered daily over the crevices like gold
Yet we ask no compensation for our destruction.
And with our precious bodies we cover the swamps.[10]

Jerusalem

by Y. Fichman

Jerusalem! Cry of the hungry heart, oblivion's
garden beyond the hills when refugees fled the storm—
Silence you are, submission and rebellion.
Because of you, heart shudders, the griefs swarm.

By green of your earth I swear and by your sunlight,
I inherit the desolation that remains.
I should like a tree in stone; by you held spellbound—
soul woven with soul, my root in your dry veins.

[10] Mintz, *Modern Hebrew Poetry*, pp. 120–22.

I love what survives in you as in cold lava,
The rejoicing sound of ancient days,
echoing still from your white rocks of silence.

But with your holiness is now my strife,
And I have come to smash rocks into clods.
Dead splendor rests on furrows of new life.[11]

Not all the poets who wrote of Jerusalem actually emigrated to Palestine. Some, like Leivick, went from Russia to the United States and wrote in Yiddish.

On Your Earth, Jerusalem

by H. Leivick

On your earth, Jerusalem
I can be silent for ages.
I open for my words
All their cages.

I let them all
Go out free,
With thanks and with praise
For their loyalty.

I release them—"Go
Over all the mountains," I say.
"Over all the hills of Jerusalem,
My dear ones, fly away.
Choose the holiest places—
They are all your own.
Go, rest there, rest.
Leave me here, alone,
With the dream that I dream,
To be for one minute, at least
With myself at peace."

"On your earth, Jerusalem,
The silence goldens by day.

[11] S. Y. Penueli and A. Ukhmani, eds., *Anthology of Modern Hebrew Poetry* (Jerusalem: Institute for the Translation of Hebrew Literature, 1966), 1:105. All rights reserved by the author. Translator unlisted.

The silence blues at night."
I stop, and I suddenly say:
"Was it here Isaiah trod?
Was it really here?"

The night-silence answers:
"Yes, it was here he stood."
Baffled, I call to my words,
I call them back like birds:
"Return, my dear ones, from your places.
Help me in silence to rejoice,
That here where Isaiah trod,
My foot now paces." [12]

"I never saw you, my city, but you were for me reality seen
in dream," wrote another Yiddish poet, Israel Emmiot.

At my cradle with the little goat of gold
And the almonds and raisins that I was told
Would be the reward for studying Torah,
My mother's one dream for me of old,
You too stood there, my town.
And in the *heder,* in winter nights
As sad as my rabbi's chant where he
Wonderfully sorrowfully
Over the death of Mothel Rachel wept,
You stood, Jerusalem, so close to my heart.
Where do you, wonderful city, start? . . .

Later I knew you from the old collecting stamps
For the funds to help the pious pilgrims in Jerusalem,
Three trees weeping by the Wailing Wall,
Weeping like my birch-trees here
That sway in the autumn-wind by the cross-roads.

Is nothing more left, father dear,
Than this wall here,
And the trees that grow out of it?
Nothing more, my child, nothing more at all.

[12] Joseph Leftwich, ed. and trans., *The Golden Peacock* (New York:
Thomas Yoseloff, 1961), pp. 124–25.

Yet when a book came
from Jerusalem,
Because we stinted ourselves bread
And sent a few coins to the fund
For the pious pilgrims living in Jerusalem,
And he saw the words printed on
The title page—"Jerusalem, the holy town,"
His shrunken face with the bones showing through
Lighted up with an astonishing light,
And his old dim eyes shone bright:
"Come here, my son, look at this,
"A new book from Jerusalem, come here and these pages kiss." [13]

Meanwhile, Nobel laureate S. Y. Agnon recorded the growing Jewish malaise in Jerusalem under the British Mandate.

On the even of new moon, I walked to the Wailing Wall, as we in Jerusalem are accustomed to do, to pray at the Wailing Wall at the rising of each moon.

Already most of the winter had passed, and spring blossoms had begun to appear. Up above, the heavens were pure, and the earth had put off her grief. The sun smiled in the sky; the City shone in its light. And we too rejoiced, despite the troubles that beset us; for these troubles were many and evil, and before we had reckoned with one, yet another came in its wake.

From Jaffa Gate as far as the Wailing Wall, men and women from all the communities of Jerusalem moved in a steady stream, together with those newcomers whom the Place (the Kabbalistic name for God) had restored to their place, albeit their place had not yet been found. But in the open space before the Wall, at the booth of the Mandatory Police, sat the police of the Mandate, whose function it was to see that no one guarded the worshipers save only they. Our adversaries, wishing to provoke us, perceived this and set about their provocations. Those who had come to pray were herded together and driven to seek shelter close up against the stones of the Wall, some weeping and some as if dazed. And still we say, How long, O Lord? How long? For we have trodden the lowest stair of degradation, yet You tarry to redeem us.

I found a place for myself at the Wall, standing at times amongst

[13] *Ibid.,* pp. 480–81.

the worshipers, at times amongst the bewildered bystanders. I was amazed at the peoples of the world; as if it were not enough that they oppressed us in all lands, yet they must also oppress us in our home.[14]

After the 1948 War of Liberation, Jerusalem was partitioned and Jews lost access to the Old City and all their holy places. After the first cease-fire Dov Joseph, the officer in charge of Jerusalem, took a walk through the New City, dismissing from his mind "the thought of the destruction he could not see in the Jewish Quarter of the Old City of Jerusalem." He described this in his book *The Faithful City*.[15]

As one walked through the streets one's eye took note of broken glass, bits of red tiles of roofs, pieces of wood of all descriptions strewn about, torn telephone and electric wires along the roadsides, the parched dry earth of the open spaces, trees cut as though by a giant saw, large branches of uprooted trees across the pavements and in the road. Twisted shutters, broken windows and piles of broken glass decorated a city crowned with broken tiled roofs and splintered beams sticking out of the roofs. Where an outer staircase had been blown away a ladder had been substituted. Fortunately Jerusalem is a city of stone, so that most of the walls of the houses stood up well to the shelling, but the walls had gaping holes in them and as one entered the houses it was a different picture—plaster, broken furniture, and pieces of shell still stuck in the walls or the dusty floors. Many houses showed signs of direct hits, some by incendiary bombs so that the outer walls were blackened and the houses themselves burned out.

In the bright summer sunshine all this seemed like a modern abstract painting hanging crookedly on a nail in an open courtyard. But I knew, only too well, that each physical sign of destruction had been accompanied by human suffering. The shelling had been heaviest during the last days when negotiations for the truce had been in process. The shelling had not let up at all. The punishment of

[14] Reprinted by permission of Schocken Books Inc., from S. Y. Agnon, "Tehila," trans. Walter Lever, *Israeli Stories,* ed. Joel Blocker (New York: Schocken Books, 1962), pp. 29–30. Copyright © 1962 by Schocken Books Inc.

[15] Copyright © 1960, by Dov Joseph. Reprinted by permission of Simon & Schuster, Inc.

Jerusalem had been by systematic mortar fire, a kind of combing out
of the city from one end to the other. Not a single quarter had been
spared. It had been the climax of the effort to wear down our resistance in the hope that surrender would take the place of the truce
being negotiated.

To the surprise of all except the few who remembered how truly
stiff-necked are the Jews, there had been no general panic and no
widespread desire to surrender. After all the terrible days of tension
and strain, of personal disaster and pain, I tried to forget what might
come after this truce, and my mind was already busy with the work
of rebuilding. At the same time my eyes followed with pleasure the
sight of children venturing out, for the first time in many weeks, into
the street, women hanging out their bedding for a much-needed
airing, boys trading in pieces of shrapnel. Men were conspicuous by
their absence; slowly they would be given a chance to come home to
see what had happened while they were on duty in other parts of
the city. As the sights of destruction were filled in with human forms
the picture changed, and I could say to myself, "How goodly are thy
tents, O Jacob," even those smashed by the Arab Legion's fire.

At the end of the fighting, in March, 1949, Joseph subsequently
became Military Governor of Jerusalem. He concludes his account:

This story must end where it began, with the city of Jerusalem.
More than ever before, it had become, for me as for all the Jews of
Israel, the living memorial of our history. We knew that what we
were living through was no more than a page in that long history,
but it was a new page, filled with words of new hope. So Jerusalem
in the summer of 1948 was more than the citadel of our ancient
glories; it had become the symbol of our future.

During the second truce, I found myself once in a curious but
revealing argument, late at night in my home, with one of the
United Nations observers. He was a good friend of mine, a man of
great ability and courage, a good Catholic. When I pressed him for
a straight answer as to what he would be prepared to sacrifice for
Jerusalem—the city itself and not the idea—he admitted that it was
not worth the little finger of one of his children's hands. I could
not help thinking of the words of the mother of a Jewish soldier
who had been killed in the fight for Mount Zion, a devout Jewess,
who said, "I shall go down to my grave mourning my son, but if

his death helped in a small way to save the city the sacrifice is not too great."

Harry Levin's diary gives an even more moving account of the same events.

April 26 (1948)   Shimon and I talked of the British, whom he thinks he understands, of the Arabs, whom he really understands, of Hebrew literature, which he teaches, and foreign literature, which he studies. But we spoke especially of Jerusalem. He was born in Safed, but has lived here since boyhood. . . . Shimon spoke of Jerusalem as a lover speaks of his bride. Even the four softly-falling syllables, *Yerushalayim,* when he pronounced it, held a world of feeling.

I cannot love Jerusalem the way he does. Its traditions are part of me, but as a city it is too remote and melancholy, too weighted down with the hatreds, fanaticisms, bloodshed of thousands of years. I feel that I live here within a kind of halo, woven of splendor and majesty, fed by a deep inner fire but with scant promise of earthly warmth or serenity.

May 19   My thoughts turned back to the Old City across the ravine. How would it emerge from all this? . . . Not a city as much as a symbol of the passionate beliefs, prayers, hopes of mankind through the centuries. Benedictions that have been poured over it, and the blasphemies! The emperors who have desired it—with little Abdullah of Transjordan the latest of the line! Beyond the ramparts that ancient rulers built to hold it, its fingers flicked out far beyond this land. . . .

But for the people of Old Jerusalem who live there it is still a city. Their roots and homes, their children's schools, their livelihoods are there, the treasures of their faiths. Every man living in Old Jerusalem feels himself the guardian of his faith, whatever it may be. Nowhere in the world is any man more jealous of that privilege than he. . . . The tightly-bound little Jewish Quarter, walled within the wider walls. Mixture of splendor and debris, huddle of synagogues and houses of sacred learning, squeezed beside and on top of each other; blue-washed dwellings with Rembrandt interiors, flush with narrow sordid lanes.

Whenever disturbance breaks out in Jerusalem, it starts in the Old City. When there is tension, the first place one avoids is the

Old City. And of all restrictions of movement the one you resent most is that on the Old City. For some Jews it means denial of access to the Wailing Wall. For me, denial of access to the relics of ancient ways; forgotten years that still live on here as though nothing had happened since; old streets where every stone seems hardened with age and every crevice seems to hide a secret where men live with their God behind furtive mildewed walls in strange corners not of this world. Grace, beauty, color, sordidness, magnificences amid endless confusion.

May 29—Midday There is a motionless haze over the Old City, like a ghastly jelly. Only the nearer skyline is smudged with smoke and shimmering with heat. All the colors have disappeared; the habitual blue, pink, green, all are grey now. A great silence and solitude enwrap it. Out of the haze a single smoke spiral has pushed its way upward, very tall and slender and elegant. I picture the crackling flames below it, the stones turning back.

Hard to think of the Old City without a single Jew. When last was there such a time? Nearly eight hundred years ago Maimonides found Jews there. The old underground Synagogue of Yoḥanan ben Zakkai is reputed to have been standing nearly two thousand years ago; now, like the neighboring Ḥurva, it is a shambles. Jews were in the Old City when the Seljuks conquered it, and in the days of the Crusades, and when the Turks took it over. Allenby found them when he conquered it from the Turks. But today not one is left.

I watched the refugees arrive at the once elegant Park Lane Hotel in Katamon; from there they will be distributed among the Katamon houses. Some had not seen the sun for weeks, hardly ventured out of their Old City cellars even into the darkness of the night. Only the children seemed to be living in the present. They streamed in by the hundreds, older ones holding younger brothers and sisters by the hand. They sat there in the sunshine, some in speechless misery, others just solemn and quiet, absorbing the relative freedom from terror, their eyes taking in this strange new world of modern houses. Most of the adults were not even sad, just stupefied and exhausted. Their yellow, bloodless faces and lean hands moved in slow motion. But some were utterly broken. . . .

May 3 Another day of merciless shelling. Both the Legion and Egyptians are said to have brought up new guns. The main battle for Jerusalem may be going on at Latrun, but they have decided, it seems, to demolish the city in the meantime. I heard a man say, "Our Jerusalem is melting." Every day it becomes a bit more mutilated.

A city loses its character in war, it becomes a snare; death and survival alone have meaning. But Jerusalem is not just another city. War here is pure madness; obscene, arrogant madness. And as they wage it, this is not war. They are not fighting for it, not risking even their precious tanks now. They sit on the hills, pump shells into it, into every street and corner, and mangle it. The city the world calls Holy!

These first daylight hours are free of shelling. The air is beautifully cool. In the fresh sunlight the city looks like a place of peace. God, what beauty there is in quiet! [16]

Following the War of Liberation, the Old City was in the hands of Jordan, and the New City was held by the State of Israel. The question of the future of Jerusalem—its possible internationalization as a city sacred to Christians and Jews, as well as to Moslems—was a frequent item on the agenda of the United Nations.

In an address before the Ad Hoc Political Committee of its General Assembly on November 25, 1949, Moshe Sharett, the first Foreign Minister of the new state, alluded to the ancient role of Jerusalem in Jewish life.

The historical associations which have made Jerusalem so uniquely renowned are the common property of civilized mankind. The name of that city has through the ages evoked the religious veneration of multitudes in most parts of the world. Yet universal reverence should not serve to overshadow the consuming passion of one particular attachment. To millions of men in many centuries and different climes Jerusalem has been a source of spiritual inspiration. To the Jewish people, as a people, it has been and is the very heart—the symbol of the past glory, the lodestar in its wanderings, the subject of its daily prayers, the goal of its hopes for eventual redemption.

[16] Reprinted by permission of Schocken Books Inc. from Harry Levin, *I Saw the Battle of Jerusalem* (New York: Schocken Books, 1950). Copyright © 1950 by Harry Levin.

The following February, Abba Eban eloquently reviewed the events connected with the siege of Jerusalem in an address before the Trusteeship Council of the United Nations.

The Jews of Jerusalem, engulfed in death and famine, fighting against dire odds for sheer survival itself, had little time [during the siege of 1948] to reflect on the deliberations of those who had promised them "security, well-being, peace and order," but five months ago. The Security Council, the Trusteeship Council and the General Assembly had left them no room for misunderstanding. Their alternative was now clear. They must either sit back, paralyzed and inert, while military conquest, anarchy and starvation engulfed their homes; or they must summon up their own energies to fight for their homes and their future at Israel's side. They chose the latter course. When their prospect of survival hung on a thread, at a time when parents wondered if they would see their children wither from famine before their eyes, the lifeline thrown from the State of Israel reached the beleaguered city. On the first trucks of the convoys reaching the city with water and food were inscribed the Hebrew words "If I forget thee, O Jerusalem, may my right hand forget its cunning." The people of Jerusalem were not forsaken or alone.

Once bare survival was assured and the siege heroically broken, there began a rehabilitation which has sustained its momentum ever since. In that process a relationship grew up between the State of Israel and Jewish Jerusalem which has now reached full and organic integration. It is a relationship of duty and sacrifice; of mutual responsibility and common aspiration. . . .

The people of Israel and the Jewish people throughout the world are deeply inspired by the restoration of Israel's independent life in Jerusalem in fulfillment of ancient prophecy. At the same time the solution of the question of the Holy Places in a universal spirit is a purpose which we ardently uphold. While the Christian and Moslem Holy Places were mercifully spared serious damage, the ancient synagogues in the Old City were wantonly destroyed after the end of hostilities. . . .

I am aware that there are some throughout the Christian world who still sincerely doubt whether the destiny of modern Jerusalem as the center of Israel's independence can be harmonized with

Jerusalem's universal mission. To them I would suggest that the existence of political freedom in Jerusalem side by side with an international authority for the Holy Places is not only a more expedient and practical solution than that envisaged in the Statute. It is also in every sense a higher ideal. It was as the center of an active political and cultural life, beset by the problems and ordeals of a State, that Jerusalem in antiquity became the home of prophecy and revelation. Only a city alive with movement and ideas could have attracted to its midst the searching minds and spirits who generalized transient events into abiding truths. Prophecy and spiritual searchings have never flourished in a museum. They only arise out of the issues and dilemmas of life. The spiritual heritage which has gone forth from Jerusalem is historically linked with its character as a political center, and with the ancient people who established Jerusalem on what was an obscure Jebusite hill. Surely a sensitive religious insight cannot fail to see some grandeur in the restoration of this people to the city which its own experience rendered famous in the world. . . .

Our vision is of a Jerusalem wherein a free people develops its reviving institutions, while a United Nations representative, in all tranquility and dignity, fulfills the universal responsibility for the safety and accessibility of the Holy Places. This is a vision worthy of the United Nations. Our Organization should move at once to realize this harmony and liberate its energies for the issues affecting human survival. Perhaps in this as in other critical periods of history a free Jerusalem may proclaim redemption to mankind.[17]

[17] Abba Eban, *Voice of Israel* (New York: Horizon Press, 1957) pp. 50 ff. Used by permission of the publisher.

Chapter Seven

THE SIX-DAY WAR

When the Six-Day War began on Monday, June 5, 1967, the Israelis believed that Jordan, despite its recently signed pact with Egypt, would act as it had during the Sinai Campaign of 1956 and refrain from launching an attack. Jewish Jerusalem, accordingly, made no extraordinary preparations for war. However, early that same morning several residential sections in New Jerusalem were shelled. Israel did not retaliate until Jordan's intentions became clear with the invasion by her forces of Government House, the headquarters of the United Nations Truce Supervision Organization, located on the Hill of Evil Counsel, a gateway to southern Jerusalem.

By midday the Legionnaires had launched attacks along Jerusalem's entire frontier. Compelled to defend the Jewish sections of Jerusalem, the Israelis ordered their forces to open an offensive against the Old City.

Teddy Kolleck, Mayor of Jerusalem, issued the following message to the citizens of Jerusalem:

> You, the inhabitants of our Holy City, were called upon to suffer the vicious onslaught of the enemy, while our determined airmen and soldiers were battling with him in the air and in the south. Your homes also became a battlefield.
>
> In the course of the day I traveled throughout Jerusalem. I saw how its citizens, rich and poor, veteran and new immigrant alike, children and adults, stood steadfast. Nobody flinched; nobody failed. You remained cool, calm and confident, while the enemy launched his assault upon you.
>
> You have proved worthy inhabitants of the City of David. You have proved worthy of the words of the Psalmist: "If I forget thee,

O Jerusalem, may my right hand forget its cunning." You will be remembered for your stand in the hour of danger.[1]

Early on Tuesday morning (June 6), the Israeli troops moved toward the Old City; some of the fiercest battles of the war ensued, resulting in heavy casualties. Meanwhile, Jewish Jerusalem suffered heavy damage. By Wednesday, after fierce house-to-house and hand-to-hand combat, and in spite of being severely hampered by the Army's orders to protect the holy shrines, Israeli soldiers captured the Old City.

Moments after the liberation of the Western Wall, the Chief Chaplain of the Israel Defense Army addressed the troops.

> Soldiers of Israel, most cherished of the people, crowned with strength and victory. The Lord is with you, heroes. I address you from the square before the Wall, the remnant of our Temple. Be comforted, be comforted my people, says your God. This is the day which the Lord has made: Let us be glad and rejoice in His victory.
>
> Today you have fulfilled the age-old oath: "If I forget thee, O Jerusalem, may my right hand lose its cunning." Indeed, we have not forgotten Jerusalem, our Holy City and glorious home. Your right hand, the right hand of the Lord, has wrought this historic liberation.
>
> The vision of generations has been realized in our presence. The city of God, the Temple site, the Temple Mount and the Western Wall, the symbols of our people's Messianic redemption, were this day liberated by you, heroes of Israel's Defense Army.
>
> Whose heart does not exalt or rejoice upon hearing this message of redemption? From this day forward Zion's gates and those of the Old City and the roads to the Western Wall are open for the prayers of Zion's children—builders and redeemers, those in *Eretz Yisrael* and those outside it—let them come and make pilgrimages here and beseech God, the Creator of the Universe, at this site.
>
> The *Shekhinah*, which has never departed from the Western Wall, walks ahead of the Israeli forces as a pillar of fire to illumine the path of victory, and bedecks us with clouds of glory in the presence of our people and the nations of the world. Happy are we who have been granted this sublime moment, the most exalted in our people's history.

[1] *Jerusalem Post,* June 6, 1967.

To the nations of the world we declare: With reverence and dignity we will respect the shrines hallowed by all faithful, peace-loving people; these shrines shall be open to members of all religions.

Soldiers and dear children! By your deeds the entire nation has been deemed worthy of this great event. The prophetic visions and ancient prayers are being fulfilled. "You, O Lord, did consume her with fire, and with fire You will in the future rebuild her, as it is said: 'I will be to her, says the Lord, a wall of fire round about, and for glory I will be in her midst' (Zechariah 2:9). We praise You, O Lord, Comforter of Zion and Builder of Jerusalem."

To Zion and the Temple remnant we declare: your sons have returned to their borders, our feet stand within your gates, Jerusalem, a city that is compact together, a city which has been reunited with new Jewish Jerusalem. This is the city that men called the perfection of beauty, the joy of the whole earth, the capital city of the State of Israel.

In the name of the entire Jewish people, those in Israel and those in the Diaspora, I recite: "We praise You, Lord our God, King of the universe, who has granted us life and sustained us and enabled us to reach this hour."

Shortly after, Prime Minister Levi Eshkol sent a message to the people of Israel from the Wall.

It is a great and historic privilege to stand here this hour, beside the Western Wall, the relic of our sacred Temple and our historic past. I regard myself as a representative of many generations of our people, whose souls have yearned for Jerusalem and its sanctity.

To the people of Jerusalem who suffered severely in 1948, and who have held their own, with valor and unflinching calm, against the malicious bombardments of the past few days, let me say: the victories of the Israel Defense Forces, which will remove the danger from Israel's capital, will be a source of encouragement and consolation to you and to all of us. In the consolation of Jerusalem may you find consolation.

And from Jerusalem, Israel's eternal Capital, I send a greeting of peace to all Israel's citizens and to our Jewish brethren wherever they may be.

Praised be He that has granted us life and sustained us and enabled us to reach this hour.

The soldiers themselves realized they were participating in one of the most amazing episodes in Jewish history: the fulfillment of a dream nurtured for millennia. In one of the most eloquent documents to come out of the Six-Day War, a collection of letters and statements by kibbutz soldiers entitled *Siaḥ Loḥamim* (*Soldiers Talking*).[2] one soldier wrote to a friend on August 20, 1967:

> I was privileged to serve in the paratrooper squadron that liberated Jerusalem. I believe that my participation in the liberation of Jerusalem was the result of God's intervention. I see it as a divine act because ever since I became a man, but especially since I was drafted almost thirteen years ago, I yearned to have the privilege of taking part in Jerusalem's redemption. No doubt this contradicts my socio-political views about the necessity for dialogue with the Arabs in order to create a basis for peace. However, the overwhelming desire to take part in Jerusalem's deliverance overshadows all political ideologies. . . .
>
> Instead of feeling fear and dread at the prospect of death, I experienced a warm glow. A wonderful joy enveloped me when I realized that I was about to fight, and perhaps die, for Jerusalem. Can anyone grasp the full significance of Jerusalem for a believing Jew, who thrice daily prays, "Return in mercy to Your city Jerusalem and dwell in it as You have promised . . ." ?
>
> As you indicated, I never regarded the Western Wall as an archeological site nor even what many call a "holy shrine." My training, prayers and dreams wove Jerusalem in its entirety as an inextricable fiber of my life and personality. Try to understand that that is how I felt when I went to fight to liberate Jerusalem. I felt as if a great privilege had been granted me, a divine, historic mission. The tensions and din of battle left little time to speculate about my comrades' feelings. Yet, there was the sense of a great and sacred moment in the air. Standing together in the Rockefeller Museum, I asked one of my buddies from Kibbutz Shaar Haamaqim, "Well, what do you have to say about it all?" At once he quoted this Biblical verse: "I rejoiced when they said unto me: 'Let us go unto the house of the Lord'; Our feet are standing within your gates, O Jerusalem: Jerusalem that is built as a city that is compact together . . ." He smiled as he recited the verse (Psalms 122:1–3). Perhaps

---

[2] An English edition entitled *The Seventh Day*, translated by Henry Near, is scheduled to appear in the summer of 1970. See Further Readings.

he sensed it was "out of place" for a member of Hashomer Hatzair to speak this way. But I could see in his eyes that that was the way he felt.

When we broke through to the Old City and I climbed up to the Temple Mount, and later when I went to the Western Wall I saw officers and soldiers weeping as I watched them praying wordlessly. Then I knew that they felt exactly as I did; they shared the same profound attachment to the Temple Mount on which the Temple stood, and the same love for the Wall at whose stones generations of Jews had wept. Then, too, I realized that not only my "religious" friends and I sense the grandeur and the holiness, but so do they, and with equal cogency and depth. It was simpler for me to give vent to my feelings because I had my *tefillin* in my belt (perhaps, King Solomon had once worn a similar pair) and I carried the Book of Psalms, composed by David, King of Jerusalem.

As I wept at the Wall my father, grandfather, and great-grandfather joined me. All of them had been born in *Eretz Yisrael,* but they had needed Abdullah's permission to pray there. When I hugged the stones of the Wall I felt the warmth of the Jewish hearts that had been inflamed by the Wall, whose ardor will endure forever. . . .

I beheld several of my buddies who ostensibly had lacked all feelings of holiness, who had been reared to denigrate traditional religious values, now as jubilant and excited as I was. Then I knew what I had previously only assumed, that there is something in us Jewish people. In the so-called "secular" as in the "religious" Jew there is a profound Jewish quality that can never be uprooted, nor can alien values or ideals distort it.

The morning after the battle I recited my morning prayers on the Temple Mount. I especially emphasized the verse: "O cause a new light to shine upon Zion, and may we all be worthy soon to enjoy its brightness."

I apologize if I have been too sentimental. But everything surrounding the Six-Day War, and especially the liberation of Jerusalem, seems to me so poetic and hymnal.[3]

Excerpts in the same volume from statements by other soldiers throw additional light on the attitudes of young Israelis, "religious" and "non-religious" toward Jerusalem.

[3] *Siah Lohamim,* ed. Avraham Shapiro (Tel Aviv: Hatenuah Hakib-butzit, 1968), pp. 240–41. My translation.

Lotan: I was not a member of the battalions which captured Jerusalem. But I think we must differentiate between Jerusalem and the other territories. As regards the latter, we ought to remain there for as long as the national security dictates. In my opinion, however, once the security problems are solved, we have no right to remain in those areas which we won by force. It matters little who started the war and in what circumstances. But I do not say the same about Jerusalem. Jerusalem has much deeper meaning for me . . . it is something of the heart . . . it is emotional . . . I know that it was the source, it was the corner-stone for all Jews . . . Jerusalem symbolizes our entire history. It traverses our history. It was the focus of our existence. Jerusalem is more than a concept . . . it is a cosmos that contains everything.[4]

Shimon: When the soldiers came up to the Wall they were no longer cynics. The men approached and touched the stones, sighing and breathing heavily. There was something about it. . . . True, we were part of a historical situation. . . . We should not forget that we arrived at the Wall on the day the war ended. It was the climax of the war. When I touched the Wall's stones I knew the war was over . . . at that second the war ended. . . .

Amram: You stopped there on your way home?

Shimon: Yes. . . . We had only to get home . . . to be released and return home. . . . There was something extraordinary about it all. . . . Suddenly, to enter the Old City of Jerusalem, to see the Wall . . . it was like a dream. . . . It was other-worldly. . . . I couldn't believe it was real, that I was seeing real things. . . . Long ago I had severed my emotional ties with the holy places on the other side of the borders. I had been estranged. . . .

Amram: The Wall touched you most?

Shimon: The Wall, above all because of the circumstances and the description of its capture we had heard on the radio. . . . One sensed in the broadcast the soldiers' ecstasy—it was contagious . . . it seized us . . . we went there on the same day . . . you felt it affected the entire nation. It had ignited a spark that had been flickering deep in all our hearts and which suddenly became a flame. I remember one observant soldier telling me on that day: "The minute the war's over I'm going to Jerusalem to pray near the Wall."

[4] P. 14.

Amram: Curiously, someone from Neot Mordekhei said today he had felt the same way . . . he was sitting at home and listening to the broadcast about the Wall . . . two days after the war ended—The first thing he did was to get on a bus and ride to Jerusalem. He said he felt that he had to be at that place, to pray, to live the experience of every observant Jew at that place. He's been there twice since. . . . At times he realizes the fervor is waning.[5]

Shai: We were aware of the battles on the West Bank and of the fact that Jerusalem was being encircled. Actually, as a result of the radio broadcasts, we felt that they were about to take Jerusalem—but it did not affect us. While riding on the buses from Gaza we listened to the radio. The announcer interrupted the program and relayed the army's report that the Old City of Jerusalem was in our hands. He repeated it, and then they played "Jerusalem the Golden." I recall that we were so struck that the entire regiment broke out in song. I remember, too, that several men wept unashamedly. I know that this was the greatest moment of the war . . . this was the climax of the war . . . it epitomized the whole war. It seems to me this was not a religious expression; but when I try to explain it to myself, I can't. . . . The city has to be ours. . . . It is our capital city . . . it symbolizes something that had been taken from us.[6]

A poem in completely modern idiom is *Jerusalem Is Everyman's* by Ḥaim Ḥefer.

Take a day off. Take two of them,
Put old shoes on, dark specs, wide hat with a shady brim,
Catch a train or a bus, or borrow a bike,
And alone, with a group, or a friend you like,
Go up and seek the peace of Jerusalem.

Quietly go, tip-toe, follow him,
That paratrooper telling his girl all he's been through,
How he fought like a lion, and overcame, and advanced,
What he felt all along, and what he suddenly sensed,
What the fellows in camp whispered at midnight,
And what they bragged about in broad daylight . . .

[5] Pp. 68–69.
[6] Pp. 224–25.

And see how she gazes adoring, and swallows him whole.
    Of this
There is no doubt—Jerusalem is his.

Come to the lanes of the market where the selling has begun,
And Ovadia, Abdullah, Geula, Jamailla
Are bargaining with fury.
And Mr. Mizraḥi says: "What if we too get used to a life
    without hurry
And find this kind of life is fun?"
And he settles down to his coffee, calling the waiter:
"Ho, there, let's have a nargillah now, or a little later."
And slowly he sniffs and tastes and sighs with deep content,
And buttonholes an Arab neighbor and starts an argument.
While underfoot a merchant of seven years or so
Offers you his Chinese crayons and other wares;
And his brother shouts: "One lira!" until your ear drums blow!
And Rabinowitz buys a cake of soap, and stares:
It's Lux soap with divinely perfumed scent,
And you know
Beyond all doubt—Jerusalem is theirs.

Go through Zion's Gate and on to the Western Wall,
And jostle a black-cloaked Ḥasid and a soldier armed to
    the teeth,
Look into their eyes and see how they smile and they weep,
And see how true faith prevails over precepts after all.
Ah, here comes a deacon or gabbai; whoever he is
There's no denying—Jerusalem is his.

Look, the city inspectors are taking the measure of
    crooked lanes,
See how they stop to record all manner of curious signs
    and names.
Here are some workers tearing down barriers, fences and
    wire,
There is a bulldozer crashing through rubble and broken
    stone halls,
And razing a hutment that clings like a leech to the
    Old City walls.
And now, as the sun rises higher,

Teddy Kollek arrives, breathing hard, chest heaving,
No wonder! He has to make all Jerusalem a Festival City.
Here a waterpipe is leaking,
There a street sadly needs cleaning,
Everywhere red tape must be slashed without pity.

The bulldozer driver catches sight of the Mayor
Out of the tail of his eye.
In a flash he makes a house vanish in air,
And marvels to see the dust fly.
And thinks: "What an excellent job this is!"
Why not? Is not Jerusalem his?

A bell rings out. On a roof three monks appear.
The church flags wave in a cloud as if a holiday is here.
In the Via Dolorosa, basket on arm, a nun passes by,
Glancing at the Jews with a cold blue eye.
She goes through an iron gate and into her house of prayer,
And eyes with disdain a photographer loitering there.
And this occurs
Because of course—Jerusalem is hers.

Evening gathers, and the shadows of the houses lengthen,
And round about Jerusalem the blue Judean mountains redden,
In the sunset glow.
And as the shades of night upon the city fall,
It is good, O how very good, that the world should know
That our Jerusalem belongs to all.[7]

In 1967, for the first time in Jewish history, Tishah Be'av, the
day of fasting when Jews mourn the destruction of the Temple,
was not a time for lamentation.

    Ḥasidim with long curls and black caftans and sneakers danced
up the winding hills. Youngsters laughed. Orthodox women, their
arms and legs and heads covered, talked happily and busily. . . .
    Suddenly we were upon it—the Wall itself. Thousands and thou-
sands of people were massed before it. The whole Diaspora of
Jews was joined together. Men were praying in tiny groups as they
had prayed in communities in Africa and Asia, in the little vil-

    [7] Trans. Sylvia Satten Banin, *Wizo Review,* no. 137 (Summer, 1967),
p. 7.

lages of Europe, for hundreds of years. The Yemenites sat in a circle on the floor; they sang and swayed. In Yemen, they were not allowed to ride on camels; they had defied their oppressors by rocking back and forth on their dream camels.

The Ḥasidim shook and danced in ecstasy. A soldier with a stump for a leg leaned his crutch on the bridal-white Wall and prayed alone in silence. A group of soldiers draped their prayer shawls on their heads, and prayed together—thankful that they were whole.[8]

For sensitive Jews the world over, the reunification of Jerusalem seemed to blend the past with the immediate present, and both took on fresh meaning as elements that had been predicted in the Messianic visions of the future. All the epochs of Jewish existence and Jerusalem's saga merged together to forge an apocalyptic presence. The barriers between dream and reality were shattered as barricades between the Old and New Cities were demolished. Geographic borders were surmounted, and individual ideologies seemed insignificant. The natural receded before the supernatural, the empirical gave way to the miraculous. Celestial Jerusalem seemed to merge with its terrestrial counterpart.

The wheel had come full circle. Jewish Jerusalem had again been linked with its Biblical antecedents, its ancient shrines, and its hallowed memories.

There are seven gates in the wall of the Old City of Jerusalem, and each one of them is different from the others—in the appearance of its towers, in its ornaments and decorations, in its position against the mountainscape. Each of them has a splendor of its own. But the most splendid of all is the eighth gate, the one that is not in use at all, whose opening has been sealed for many a generation with layers of heavy stones. The double-arched façade of this gate is discernible in all its splendor from afar; but the gate itself is blind, impenetrable. Its name is "Gate of Mercy." Some call it the Golden Gate, or Gate of Eternal Life.

The sealed gate is built into the eastern wall of the Old City, on the heights of Mount Moriah. Beyond it, to the west, is the

[8] Ruth Gruber, *Israel on the Seventh Day* (New York: Hill & Wang, 1968), pp. 198–99.

holiest of Jerusalem's holy sites—the courtyard of the ancient Temple; and, to the east, the mount slopes down into the Valley of Jehoshaphat, with the Mount of Olives rising on the opposite side of the vale.

An ancient Jewish legend—one of the thousands of legends that have permeated the stones of Jerusalem for centuries—relates that in the Latter Days all the dead that have been buried on the Mount of Olives these thousands of years will be resurrected, and others deceased the world over will likewise be restored to life and will join these multitudes here. Here, in the Vale of Jehoshaphat, all the peoples of the earth will be judged before the Lord; and the Messiah will stride at the head of a redeemed nation, the Prophet Elijah marching in front of him, sounding the Ram's Horn to herald the Messiah's advent, until the procession arrives at the sealed gate—and, lo! its layers of stone will tremble and shudder and suddenly they will topple of their own accord, and the gate will open wide to admit the Messiah and the multitude following in his wake.[9]

The legends surrounding Jerusalem are the subject of an entire novel by Elie Wiesel.

> Jerusalem: the face visible yet hidden, the sap and blood of all that makes us live or renounce life. The spark flashing in the darkness, the murmur rustling through shouts of happiness and joy. A name, a secret. For the exiled, a prayer. For all others, a promise. Jerusalem: seventeen times destroyed yet never erased. The symbol of survival. Jerusalem: the city which miraculously transforms man into pilgrim: no one can enter it and go away unchanged.
>
> For me, it is also a little town somewhere in Transylvania, lost in the Carpathians, where, captivated as much by mystery as by truth, a Jewish child studies the Talmud and is dazzled by the richness, the melancholy of its universe made up of legend. . . .
>
> Rabbi Naḥman of Bratzlav, the storyteller of Ḥasidism, liked to say that no matter where he walked, his steps turned toward Jerusalem. As for me, I discovered it in the sacred word. Without taking a single step. . . .
>
> Here is the Valley of Yehoshaphat where one day the nations

[9] Yehuda Haczraḥi, *In Jerusalem the Stones Speak*. Reprinted by permission of the author.

will be judged. The Mount of Olives, where one day death will be vanquished. The citadel, the fortress of David, with its small turrets and golden domes where suns shatter and disappear. The Gate of Mercy, heavily bolted: let anyone other than the Messiah try to pass and the earth will shake to its foundations.

And higher than the surrounding mountains of Moab and Judea, here is Mount Moriah, which since the beginning of time has lured man in quest of faith and sacrifice. It was here that he first opened his eyes and saw the world that henceforth he would share with death; it was here that, maddened by loneliness, he began speaking to his Creator and then to himself. It was here that his two sons, our forefathers, discovered that which links innocence to murder and fervor to malediction. It was here that the first believer erected an altar on which to make an offering of both his past and his future. It was here, with the building of the Temple, that man proved himself worthy of sanctifying space as God had sanctified time.

This city of unshakeable memory, I admit loving it, I even admit loving its hold over me. Distant lands no longer lure me. The seeker is weary of seeking, the explorer of self-excitement. Beneath this sky in which colors and faces clash, steps in the night reverberate to infinity; one listens, spellbound, overwhelmed. Follow them far enough and you will take by surprise a king lost in a dream, a prophet who reduces life and language to dust.[10]

Another eloquent voice lifted in praise of Jerusalem is that of Abraham Joshua Heschel in his article "Listen to the Stones of Jerusalem: An Echo of Eternity" (*Hadassah Newsletter* 49, no. 1 [Sept. 1967]: 4).

I have discovered a new land. Israel is not the same as before. There is great astonishment in the souls. It is as if the prophets had risen from their graves. Their words ring in a new way. Jerusalem is everywhere, she hovers over the whole country. There is a new radiance, a new awe.

The great quality of a miracle is not in its being an unexpected, unbelievable event in which the presence of the holy bursts forth,

[10] Reprinted by permission of Random House, Inc. from Elie Wiesel, *A Beggar in Jerusalem*, pp. 11–12. Copyright © 1970 by Elie Wiesel. See Further Readings. Translation by Lily Edelman and author.

but in its happening to human beings who are profoundly astonished at such an outburst.

My astonishment is mixed with anxiety. Am I worthy? Am I able to appreciate the marvel?

I did not enter on my own the city of Jerusalem. Streams of endless craving, clinging, dreaming, flowing day and night, midnights, years, decades, centuries, millennia, streams of tears, of pledging, waitings—from all over the world, from all corners of the earth—carried us of this generation to the Wall. My ancestors could only dream of you, to my people in Auschwitz you were more remote than the moon, and I can touch your stones! Am I worthy? How shall I ever repay these moments?

The martyrs of all ages are sitting at the gate of heaven, having refused to enter the world to come lest they forget Israel's pledge given in and for this world:

If I forget thee, O Jerusalem,

Let my right hand wither.

Let my tongue cleave to the roof of my mouth

If I do not remember you

If I do not set Jerusalem above my highest joys.

Further Readings

The following selected bibliography includes titles in English which may prove of interest to anyone wishing to pursue the subject further.

Adler, E. N., ed. *Jewish Travellers: A Treasury of Travelogues from Nine Centuries.* 2d ed. New York: Hermon Press, 1966.

The Authorized Kinnot for the Ninth of Av. Translated and annotated by Abraham Rosenfeld. London: Labworth and Co., 1965.

Daily Prayer Book. Translated and annotated by Philip Birnbaum. New York: Hebrew Publishing Co., 1949.

Ginzberg, Louis. *The Legends of the Jews.* 7 vols. Philadelphia: Jewish Publication Society of America, 1909–61. Shorter version: *Legends of the Bible.* New York: Simon & Schuster, 1956.

Halkin, Abraham S. *Zion in Jewish Literature.* New York: Herzl Press, 1961.

Heschel, Abraham J. *Israel: An Echo of Eternity.* New York: Farrar, Straus & Giroux, 1968.

The Holy Scriptures According to the Masoretic Text: A New Translation. Philadelphia: Jewish Publication Society of America, 1917.

Josephus. *The Jewish War.* Translated by G. A. Williamson. Harmondsworth, England: Penguin Books, 1959.

Kolleck, Teddy, and Moshe Pearlman. *Jerusalem: A History of Forty Centuries.* New York: Random House, 1968.

Kotker, Norman. *The Earthly Jerusalem.* New York: Charles Scribner's Sons, 1969.

Midrash Rabbah. Edited by H. Freedman and M. Simon. London: Soncino Press, 1939.

The Seventh Day. Translated by Henry Near. London: André

Deutsch, 1970. American edition: New York: Charles Scribner's Sons, forthcoming.

The Talmud. Edited by Isadore Epstein. London: Soncino Press, 1938.

The Torah: The Five Books of Moses: A New Translation of the Holy Scriptures. Philadelphia: Jewish Publication Society of America, 1962.

Wiesel, Elie. *A Beggar in Jerusalem*. Translated by Lily Edelman and author. New York: Random House, 1970.

Wilhelm, Kurt, ed. *Roads to Zion: Four Centuries of Travelers' Reports*. New York: Schocken Books, 1948.

Index

Date Due